Advanced Computational Security

Advanced Computational Security

Edited by

Dr. Rahul Sharma, Swapnil M. Parikh, Gaurav Kumar Ameta and Sumitra Menaria

ARCLER PRESS

www.arclerpress.com

Advanced Computational Security

Edited by: Dr. Rahul Sharma, Swapnil M. Parikh, Gaurav Kumar Ameta and Sumitra Menaria

Arcler Press
4164 Lakeshore Road
Burlington, ON L7L 1A4
Canada
www.arclerpress.com
Email: orders@arclereducation.com

ISBN: 978-1-77956-954-7 (Hardcover)

ABOUT THE EDITORS

Dr. Rahul Sharma, working as Assistant Professor – Senior Scale in the Department of Artificial Intelligence & Machine Learning, at Manipal University, Jaipur, Rajasthan. Prior to that he has more than 8+ years of teaching experience in several universities and engineering colleges as Assistant Professor in Department of Computer Science and Engineering at Parul Institute of Technology, Parul University Vadodara, Gujarat, Chameli Devi Group of Institution, Indore and Dr. A.P.J. Abdul Kalam University, he completed B.E. (CSE) from Patel College of Science and Technology, Indore (M.P.) and M.Tech (NM&IS) from SCSIT, DAVV, Indore (M.P.), PhD degree in Computer Science and Engineering from Rabindranath Tagore University Bhopal (M.P.). His research includes Computer Network, Network Security, Cryptography, Data Mining and Web Programming's. He is having 20+ research publications in reputed international journal, International- National conferences and 6 - patents (3 published-3 Registered). He also has qualified GATE (CSE) in 2015. He is publishing more than 30+ books in the field of computer science and Engineering.

Swapnil M. Parikh, PhD, is currently working as a Professor in the Computer Science and Engineering Department and also serves as Principal at Parul Institute of Technology, Parul University. He has also worked as Associate Dean of Doctoral Studies and Research at Parul University, Vadodara, Gujarat, India. He received his PhD (Computer Engineering) degree in 2019 from C. U. Shah University, Wadhwan, Surendranagar, India. He completed his Master of Engineering (Computer Engineering) in 2007 from Dharmsinh Desai University, Nadiad, India, and his Bachelor of Engineering in 2005 from Pune University. He has received various research grants from the Royal Academy of Engineering (UK), AICTE, and others. He has authored several research papers, which have been presented and published by prominent publishers such as Springer, IEEE, and other renowned journals. He has also published two patents. His research interests include networking, cloud computing, data science, IoT, big data, and machine learning.

Gaurav Kumar Ameta, PhD, is a passionate academician and researcher. He is presently working as an Associate Professor in the Department of Computer Science and Engineering at Parul Institute of Technology, Parul University, Vadodara, Gujarat (India). He has more than 16 years of teaching and research experience in India and abroad in various capacities. His areas of specialization are data mining, data science, machine learning, and deep learning. He completed his Doctor of Philosophy (Ph.D.) in Computer Science and Engineering with a specialization in privacy-preserving data mining from Sir Padampat Singhania University, Udaipur (Rajasthan). He has supervised more than 25 M.Tech and Ph.D. research scholars for their project and research work. He has been actively associated with IIT Mumbai and IIT Roorkee for coordinating and executing e-learning programs under the National Mission on Education through ICT (NMEICT) and Virtual Labs, respectively. He has been invited as a reviewer and advisory committee member in several international conferences and journals. He has been honored by several organizations and societies for his valuable contributions in the field of academics and research. Dr. Ameta is a lifetime member of the Computer Society of India (CSI) and the Indian Society for Technical Education (ISTE).

Sumitra Menaria, M.Tech, is working as an Assistant Professor in the Department of Computer Science and Engineering at Parul Institute of Technology, Parul University, Vadodara, Gujarat. She has over 16 years of academic experience. She completed her academic qualifications, including an M.Tech (CSE) from Nirma University, and is pursuing a PhD degree in computer science and engineering from Gujarat Technological University, Gujarat. Her research includes data science, data mining, cryptography, cybersecurity, and online social networking. She has published 15 research papers in various national and international journals and conferences.

TABLE OF CONTENTS

LIST OF FIGURES

Practical Experiments

FOREWORD

As the digital landscape continues to evolve, the importance of robust computational security cannot be overstated. *Advanced Computational Security* addresses the pressing need for innovative solutions to combat increasingly sophisticated cyber threats. In a world where data breaches, malware, and cyberattacks have become commonplace, organizations must adopt proactive measures to safeguard their assets and maintain trust.

This collection of research and insights delves into cutting-edge methodologies and technologies that enhance security protocols. It encompasses a wide range of topics, from machine learning algorithms designed for threat detection to cryptographic techniques that ensure data integrity and confidentiality. The interdisciplinary nature of this work highlights the collaboration among computer science, mathematics, and information technology, emphasizing that effective security solutions require a comprehensive understanding of both the challenges and the tools at our disposal.

Moreover, this compilation reflects the latest trends and developments in the field, showcasing innovative approaches to risk management, vulnerability assessment, and incident response. It serves as a valuable resource for researchers, practitioners, and policymakers alike, offering practical guidance and theoretical insights that can be applied across various sectors.

As we navigate an increasingly interconnected world, the contributions presented here are vital for advancing our understanding of computational security. By fostering a culture of awareness and preparedness, we can better equip ourselves to face the challenges that lie ahead. Together, we can build a more secure digital future, safeguarding our data and ensuring the integrity of our systems.

PREFACE

In the rapidly evolving landscape of digital threats, the realm of advanced computational security stands as a bastion against the rising tide of cyber risks. Prefacing this domain is an acknowledgment of the intricate interplay between cutting-edge technologies and relentless adversaries. Advanced computational security encompasses a holistic approach, blending sophisticated algorithms, robust protocols, and strategic methodologies to fortify digital fortresses. This preface delves into the ethos of proactive defense, where predictive analytics, machine learning, and artificial intelligence converge to anticipate and thwart emerging threats. It acknowledges the significance of constant vigilance, where vulnerability scanning, penetration testing, and threat intelligence serve as sentinel guardians against malicious incursions. Moreover, it underscores the imperative of collaboration and knowledge sharing within a global community striving for cyber resilience. As organizations navigate the intricate labyrinth of cyber threats, the preface to advanced computational security serves as a beacon, illuminating the path toward a safer digital future.

ACKNOWLEDGMENTS

The completion of *Advanced Computational Security* would not have been possible without the unwavering support and contributions of many individuals and organizations. We extend our heartfelt gratitude to our esteemed colleagues and contributors, whose expertise and insights have significantly enriched this work. Your dedication to advancing the field of computational security has inspired us and helped shape the discussions within this compilation.

We are particularly thankful to the researchers whose innovative ideas and findings are presented in this volume. Your willingness to share your knowledge and experiences has been invaluable in illuminating the complexities of security challenges and solutions.

We also wish to acknowledge the institutions and funding bodies that have supported our research endeavors. Your commitment to fostering collaboration and innovation in the field of cybersecurity has enabled us to explore new frontiers and address critical issues facing our digital landscape.

A special thanks goes to our editorial team for their meticulous efforts in reviewing and refining the content, ensuring that it meets the highest academic standards. Your attention to detail and constructive feedback have been crucial in bringing this work to fruition.

Lastly, we express our appreciation to our families and friends for their patience and encouragement throughout this journey. Your support has been a constant source of motivation as we strive to contribute to a more secure digital future. Together, we hope this work serves as a valuable resource for advancing knowledge and practices in computational security.

CHAPTER 1

INTRODUCTION

Contents

1.1. WHAT IS COMPUTER SECURITY?

Computer security refers to the protection of digital assets, such as hardware, software, and data, from unauthorized access, use, alteration, or destruction. It encompasses various strategies, technologies, and practices designed to safeguard computing systems and networks from threats and vulnerabilities. Figure 1.1 represents the classification of computer security services.

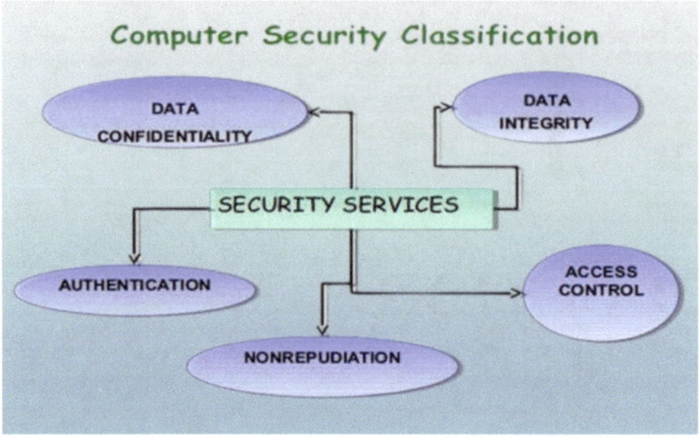

Figure 1.1. Computer security classification.

Key components of computer security include:

1. **Authentication:** Verifying the identity of users and ensuring they have appropriate access privileges.
2. **Authorization:** Determining what resources users are allowed to access and what actions they can perform.
3. **Encryption:** Encoding data to prevent unauthorized access or tampering.
4. **Firewalls:** Implementing barriers between internal networks and external networks to control incoming and outgoing traffic.
5. **Intrusion Detection Systems (IDS) and Intrusion Prevention Systems (IPS):** Monitoring network traffic for suspicious activity and taking measures to block or mitigate potential threats.
6. **Regular Updates and Patches:** Applying software updates and security patches to address known vulnerabilities.

1.1.1. Values of Assets

In the context of computer security, assets refer to any digital resources that hold value to an organization or individual. These assets can include:

1. **Data:** Information stored in databases, files, or other digital formats, such as customer records, financial data, intellectual property, and trade secrets.
2. **Hardware:** Physical devices like computers, servers, routers, and mobile devices that store or process data.
3. **Software:** Applications, operating systems, and other programs that enable users to perform tasks and manipulate data.

4. **Network Infrastructure:** Components such as routers, switches, and cables that facilitate communication between devices.
5. **Intellectual Property:** Patents, copyrights, trademarks, and other intangible assets that provide competitive advantage or generate revenue.
6. **Reputation:** The public perception of an organization's trustworthiness and reliability, which can be damaged by security breaches or data leaks.

1.1.2. The Vulnerability–Threat–Control Paradigm

The Vulnerability-Threat-Control paradigm is a foundational concept in computer security that helps understand and mitigate risks effectively.

Vulnerability refers to weaknesses or flaws in systems, networks, or applications that can be exploited by attackers to compromise security. These vulnerabilities can exist due to software bugs, misconfigurations, or inadequate security measures.

Threats are potential dangers or events that exploit vulnerabilities and can cause harm to computer systems, networks, or data. Threats can include malicious software (malware), hackers, insider threats, natural disasters, and other disruptive events.

Controls are security measures or countermeasures implemented to reduce the risk associated with vulnerabilities and threats. Controls can include technical solutions like firewalls, antivirus software, encryption, and intrusion detection systems, as well as administrative policies, procedures, and user training.

By identifying vulnerabilities, understanding potential threats, and implementing appropriate controls, organizations can effectively manage risk and enhance their overall security posture in the face of evolving cyber threats.

1.2. THREATS

Threats in the context of computer security refer to potential dangers or harmful events that can exploit vulnerabilities in systems, networks, or applications, leading to unauthorized access, data breaches, disruptions, or other adverse consequences. These threats can originate from various sources and can take numerous forms, including (Figure 1.2):

1. **Malware:** Malicious software designed to infiltrate, damage, or gain unauthorized access to computer systems or networks, such as viruses, worms, trojans, ransomware, and spyware.

2. **Hackers:** Individuals or groups with malicious intent who attempt to gain unauthorized access to systems or networks to steal data, disrupt operations, or cause damage.
3. **Insider Threats:** Employees, contractors, or other trusted individuals who misuse their privileges to access sensitive information, sabotage systems, or engage in other malicious activities.
4. **Phishing:** Deceptive techniques used to trick users into disclosing sensitive information, such as passwords or financial details, through fraudulent emails, websites, or messages.
5. **Denial-of-Service (DoS) Attacks:** Attempts to overwhelm or disrupt a system, network, or service by flooding it with excessive traffic or requests, rendering it inaccessible to legitimate users.
6. **Social Engineering:** Manipulative tactics used to exploit human psychology and trick individuals into divulging confidential information or performing actions that compromise security.
7. **Advanced Persistent Threats (APTs):** Sophisticated and targeted attacks conducted by skilled adversaries over extended periods, often with the goal of stealing sensitive data or conducting espionage.

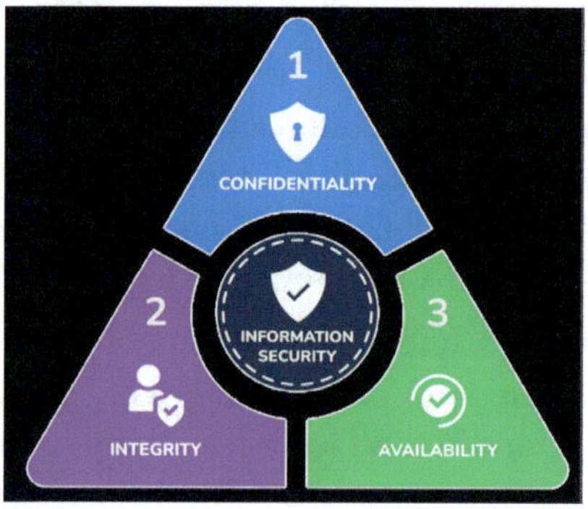

Figure 1.2. The CIA triad: Essential to cybersecurity.

1.2.1. Confidentiality

Confidentiality is a fundamental principle of information security that ensures sensitive data is accessed only by authorized individuals or entities. It involves protecting information from unauthorized disclosure or access, whether intentional or accidental. To uphold confidentiality, organizations employ various security measures, including encryption, access controls, and data classification. Encryption transforms data into an unreadable format using cryptographic algorithms, making it unintelligible to unauthorized users without the appropriate decryption key. Access controls restrict access to sensitive information based on users' roles, responsibilities, and permissions, limiting exposure to only those who have a legitimate need to know. Data classification categorizes information based on its sensitivity level, allowing organizations to apply appropriate security controls based on the data's importance and confidentiality requirements. Maintaining confidentiality is crucial for protecting sensitive information, such as personal data, financial records, trade secrets, and intellectual property. Breaches of confidentiality can lead to financial losses, reputational damage, legal repercussions, and loss of trust from customers and stakeholders. Therefore, organizations must implement robust security measures to safeguard confidential information effectively.

1.2.2. Integrity

Integrity, in the context of computer security, refers to the assurance that data remains accurate, complete, and trustworthy throughout its lifecycle. It involves protecting data from unauthorized modification, deletion, or corruption by ensuring that only authorized users can alter it and that changes are tracked and audited. To maintain data integrity, organizations implement various security measures, including access controls, cryptographic hashing, digital signatures, and data validation techniques. Access controls restrict access to data, ensuring that only authorized users can make changes. Cryptographic hashing generates unique hash values for data, allowing organizations to detect any alterations or corruption. Digital signatures provide a means to verify the authenticity and integrity of data by associating it with a unique digital signature. Data validation techniques verify the accuracy and consistency of data inputs to prevent errors and manipulation. Ensuring data integrity is essential for building trust in information systems, maintaining data accuracy, and upholding the reliability and credibility of digital assets. Breaches of data integrity can lead to erroneous decisions, financial losses, legal liabilities, and damage to organizational reputation. Therefore, organizations must implement robust integrity controls to protect against unauthorized alterations and maintain the trustworthiness of their data.

1.2.3. Availability

"Availability" in the context of advanced computing systems refers to the measure of how often a system is operational and accessible when needed. It's typically expressed as a percentage representing the amount of time a system is available compared to the total time it's expected to be available. In advanced computing systems, ensuring high availability is crucial, especially in scenarios where downtime can lead to significant losses or disruptions. Various techniques are employed to achieve high availability, including redundancy, fault tolerance, disaster recovery planning, and proactive monitoring and maintenance. Advanced computing systems often incorporate features such as load balancing, clustering, and replication to distribute workloads across multiple resources and mitigate the impact of potential failures. Additionally, technologies like virtualization and cloud computing offer scalability and resilience, further enhancing availability.

1.2.4. Types of Threats

In advanced computing systems (ACS), various types of threats can compromise the security, integrity, and availability of data and services. Figure 1.2 shows different types of cyber threats. Here are some common types of threats in ACS (Figure 1.3):

1. **Malware:** Malicious software designed to disrupt, damage, or gain unauthorized access to computer systems. This includes viruses, worms, Trojans, ransomware, and spyware.
2. **Cyberattacks:** Deliberate, targeted attempts to exploit vulnerabilities in ACS. These can include Distributed Denial of Service (DDoS) attacks, man-in-the-middle attacks, SQL injection, cross-site scripting (XSS), and zero-day exploits.
3. **Data Breaches:** Unauthorized access, disclosure, or theft of sensitive information stored in ACS. This could include personally identifiable information (PII), financial data, intellectual property, and other confidential information.
4. **Insider Threats:** Risks posed by individuals within an organization who have privileged access to ACS. This could involve employees, contractors, or partners intentionally or unintentionally compromising security through actions like data theft, sabotage, or negligence.
5. **Phishing and Social Engineering:** Deceptive techniques used to manipulate individuals into divulging sensitive information or performing actions that compromise security. Phishing emails, pretexting, baiting, and pretexting are common examples.
6. **Physical Threats:** Risks posed by physical access to ACS infrastructure. This includes theft, vandalism, natural disasters, and accidents that can damage hardware, disrupt services, or compromise data.
7. **Advanced Persistent Threats (APTs):** Sophisticated, targeted attacks by skilled adversaries aimed at gaining persistent access to ACS over an extended period. APTs often involve stealthy infiltration, reconnaissance, and lateral movement within a network.

8. **Exploitation of Vulnerabilities:** Security weaknesses in software, hardware, or configurations that can be exploited to compromise ACS. Vulnerabilities may arise from coding errors, misconfigurations, or outdated software versions.

9. **Data Loss:** Accidental or intentional deletion, corruption, or destruction of data stored in ACS. This could result from hardware failures, software errors, human error, or malicious actions.

10. **Compliance and Regulatory Risks:** Failure to comply with legal, regulatory, or industry standards governing data protection and privacy. Non-compliance with regulations such as GDPR, HIPAA, or PCI-DSS can result in legal penalties, financial losses, and reputational damage.

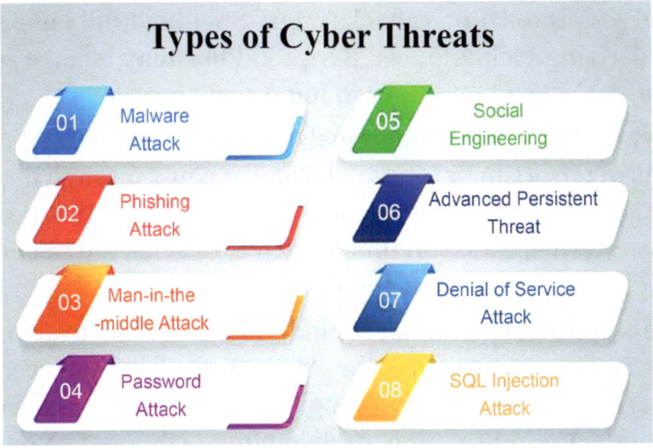

Figure 1.3. Types of cyber threats.

1.2.5. Types of Attackers

1. **Hackers:** Individuals or groups with advanced technical skills who attempt to gain unauthorized access to ACS for various purposes, including financial gain, ideological reasons, or simply the challenge of breaking into systems.

2. **Cybercriminals:** Malicious actors who engage in illegal activities for financial gain. Cybercriminals may use ACS to carry out activities such as data theft, ransomware attacks, fraud, identity theft, and selling stolen information on the dark web.

3. **State-Sponsored Actors:** Nation-states or government agencies that conduct cyber espionage, cyber warfare, or cyber terrorism against other nations, organizations, or individuals. State-sponsored

attackers may target ACS to steal sensitive information, disrupt critical infrastructure, or engage in covert intelligence gathering.

4. **Insiders:** Individuals with legitimate access to ACS who abuse their privileges for malicious purposes. Insider threats can come from disgruntled employees, contractors, or partners seeking revenge, financial gain, or to sabotage systems.
5. **Hacktivists:** Individuals or groups who use hacking techniques to promote social or political causes. Hacktivists may target ACS belonging to governments, corporations, or organizations they perceive as adversaries to disrupt operations, steal data, or deface websites as a form of protest or activism.
6. **Script Kiddies:** Inexperienced individuals who use pre-existing tools and scripts to launch attacks on ACS without fully understanding the underlying technologies. Script kiddies may engage in hacking for fun, seeking attention, or to impress their peers.
7. **Cyber Terrorists:** Individuals or groups who use ACS to carry out acts of terrorism or to spread fear and panic through the use of cyber-attacks. Cyber terrorists may target critical infrastructure, such as power grids, transportation systems, or financial networks, to cause widespread disruption and damage.
8. **Competitors:** Businesses or individuals seeking to gain a competitive advantage by targeting the ACS of rival companies. Competitors may engage in corporate espionage, stealing intellectual property, proprietary information, or disrupting operations to undermine their rivals' success.
9. **Cyber Warfare Units:** Military or intelligence agencies of nation-states that engage in offensive cyber operations against enemy nations or strategic targets. Cyber warfare units may conduct reconnaissance, launch cyber-attacks, or deploy malware to achieve military or geopolitical objectives.
10. **Opportunistic Attackers:** Individuals or automated bots scanning the internet for vulnerable ACS to exploit. Opportunistic attackers often target systems with known vulnerabilities or misconfigurations to gain unauthorized access, install malware, or use compromised resources for further attacks.

1.3. HARM

Advanced Computational Security represents the cutting-edge techniques and technologies employed to safeguard digital assets and infrastructure from cyber threats. It encompasses a multifaceted approach to securing computational systems, data, and networks through advanced algorithms, protocols, and methodologies. Encryption lies at the core of advanced computational security, ensuring that sensitive information is encoded in a manner that only authorized parties can access. Advanced encryption standards such as AES provide robust protection for data at rest and in transit. Authentication mechanisms, including multi factor authentication and biometrics, bolster security by verifying the identity of users accessing systems and data. Intrusion Detection and Prevention Systems (IDPS) play a critical role in identifying and mitigating potential threats by monitoring network traffic for suspicious activity and swiftly responding to anomalous behavior. Machine learning and artificial intelligence algorithms enhance threat detection capabilities by analyzing vast datasets to identify patterns indicative of cyber-attacks. Block chain technology is emerging as a promising tool for enhancing security through decentralized and immutable ledgers, which can enhance the integrity of transactions and data storage. Cyber threat intelligence gathering and analysis enable organizations to stay ahead of evolving threats by providing insights into emerging attack vectors and trends. Secure software development practices, such as incorporating security throughout the software development lifecycle and leveraging static and dynamic code analysis tools, are essential for building resilient applications. Additionally, robust cloud security measures tailored for cloud environments, including encryption, access control, and monitoring solutions, are vital for protecting data and applications hosted in the cloud.

1.3.1. Risk and Common Sense

To reduce risks and safeguard digital assets, advanced computational security frequently uses complex algorithms, technologies, and procedures. Recognizing the contribution of common sense to strengthening security measures is crucial, though. In advanced computational security, risk assessment is essential. It entails determining, assessing, and ranking possible threats to an organization's resources. Common sense is essential for evaluating and placing these discoveries in context, even while sophisticated technologies and procedures can help with this process by analyzing large volumes of data and spotting risks. Security experts may successfully prioritize threats and allocate resources by having a thorough understanding of the unique demands, goals, and restrictions of an organization. Using common sense is also important while putting security measures in place. Simple steps like updating software frequently, enforcing strong password policies, and warning users about phishing and social engineering attacks can greatly improve security posture—even though multifactor authentication and advanced encryption algorithms are crucial parts of a strong security strategy. Staying ahead of possible risks also requires taking a proactive approach, which involves keeping a close eye on systems for suspicious activity and acting quickly to rectify any anomalies. Moreover, common sense defines how important communication and teamwork are inside an organization. Security demands the participation of all parties involved, from executives to end users, and is not just the IT department's job. To guarantee that everyone is aware of their part in keeping the environment safe, it is important to promote a culture of security awareness and open communication.

1.3.2. Method–Opportunity–Motive

The Method-Opportunity-Motive (MOM) framework is a useful idea in advanced computational security for comprehending and reducing cyber threats. The term "method" describes the strategies and equipment that hackers employ to take advantage of weaknesses in computer systems. To identify and thwart these techniques, advanced computational security uses complex algorithms and technology, such as machine learning algorithms for anomaly detection and intrusion detection systems. Opportunity includes all of the factors that make cyberattacks possible, such as shoddy access controls, unpatched software, and poor authentication systems. Organizations can lessen the likelihood that attackers will take advantage of weaknesses by putting strong security measures in place, such as encryption, access control, and frequent software updates. The term "motive" refers to the reasons behind cyberattacks, which might include sabotage, espionage, or financial gain. Organizations can customize their security methods, such as deploying focused threat intelligence collecting and proactive defense measures, by having a clear understanding of the motivations behind prospective threats. Advanced computational security strives to counteract evolving threats to digital assets and infrastructure while reducing the effectiveness of cyberattacks by addressing the Method-Opportunity-Motive framework.

1.4. VULNERABILITIES

Advanced computational security is a multipronged strategy to address vulnerabilities in digital systems. Software faults, configuration errors, and human error are examples of vulnerabilities that greatly jeopardize the security and integrity of computing systems. Advanced computational security uses a variety of methods, including as automated vulnerability scanning, penetration testing, and code review procedures, to find and fix flaws. Large datasets are analyzed using machine learning techniques to find patterns that could point to security flaws or unusual behavior. To further guard against unauthorized access and data breaches, access control procedures and sophisticated encryption standards are put into place. Organizations are able to keep ahead of emerging vulnerabilities and quickly respond to possible attacks thanks to continuous monitoring and real-time threat intelligence gathering. Advanced computational security seeks to reduce the risk of cyberattacks and increase the resilience of digital systems by addressing vulnerabilities through proactive methods such frequent software upgrades, security patches, and employee training.

Types of vulnerabilities in cybersecurity:

1. Software Vulnerabilities: These are flaws or bugs in the code of applications or operating systems.
   - **i.** Buffer Overflow**:** Occurs when more data is written to a buffer than it can hold, potentially allowing code execution.
   - **ii.** Injection Flaws**:** Such as SQL injection, where untrusted data is sent to an interpreter as part of a command.
   - **iii.** **Cross-Site Scripting (XSS):** Allows attackers to inject malicious scripts into web pages viewed by others.
   - **iv.** Race Conditions**:** Occur when timing issues between processes allow unexpected behavior or access.
2. Hardware Vulnerabilities: Physical or design flaws in hardware components.
   - **i.** Meltdown and Specter: Exploit speculative execution in CPUs to gain access to protected memory.
   - **ii.** Firmware Vulnerabilities: Found in device firmware, often difficult to patch and exploited for persistent access.
3. Network Vulnerabilities: Related to weaknesses in protocols or configurations.
   - **i.** Open Ports: Unsecured ports that can be scanned and exploited.
   - **ii.** Unencrypted Traffic: Allows attackers to intercept sensitive data.
   - **iii.** Man-in-the-Middle (MitM) Opportunities: Due to poor authentication or encryption.
4. Configuration Vulnerabilities: Result from improper system setup.
   - **i.** Default Credentials: Systems still using default usernames and passwords.
   - **ii.** Misconfigured Firewalls or Access Controls: Allow unauthorized access.

   iii. Exposed Services: Such as databases or admin panels accessible over the internet.

5. Authentication and Authorization Flaws: Weaknesses in how users are verified and granted permissions.
   i. Weak password policies;
   ii. Broken access control;
   iii. Session management errors.
6. Human Vulnerabilities (Social Engineering): Exploiting human behavior rather than technical flaws.
   i. Phishing;
   ii. Pretexting;
   iii. Tailgating.
7. Zero-Day Vulnerabilities: Newly discovered flaws that have no patch available and are unknown to the vendor. These are especially dangerous as they can be exploited before defenses are in place.

1.5. CONTROLS

A comprehensive set of controls is necessary for advanced computational security in order to safeguard infrastructure and digital assets against online attacks. These controls include a variety of actions used to stop, identify, and handle security events. Encryption, firewalls, access control systems, and secure coding techniques are examples of preventive controls that are used to lessen the possibility of data breaches and unauthorized access. To spot any security breaches and unusual activity in real-time, detective controls including anomaly detection algorithms, log monitoring, and intrusion detection systems are used.

Additionally, disaster recovery procedures, security incident management frameworks, and incident response plans are examples of responsive controls that help organizations quickly respond to security issues and lessen their effects. Advanced computational security seeks to reduce risks and protect digital assets from a variety of cyberattacks by putting in place a tiered security architecture that combines detective, response, and preventative controls.

CHAPTER 2

TOOLBOX: AUTHENTICATION, ACCESS CONTROL, AND CRYPTOGRAPHY

Contents

2.1. AUTHENTICATION

Authentication in network security is a critical process that ensures only authorized users or devices can access network resources. It serves as the first line of defense in protecting sensitive information and maintaining the integrity of a network.

Key concepts of authentication in network security:

- **Identification and Authentication:**
    i. **Identification:** It is the process where a user or device presents credentials to the network (e.g., a username).
    ii. **Authentication:** It is the subsequent step that verifies these credentials, typically using a password, token, or biometric data, to confirm the user's or device's identity.

Types of Authentications (Figure 2.1):

i. **Password-based Authentication:** The most common form, where users authenticate by entering a secret password. The effectiveness depends on the complexity and secrecy of the password.

ii. **Two-Factor Authentication (2FA):** Enhances security by requiring two forms of identification, such as a password and a code sent to a mobile device.

iii. **Multi-Factor Authentication (MFA):** Expands on 2FA by including multiple authentication methods, such as biometrics (fingerprints, facial recognition) or physical tokens, providing an additional layer of security.

iv. **Certificate-based Authentication:** Uses digital certificates to authenticate users or devices. Each certificate is linked to a public and private key pair, ensuring secure communication and authentication.

v. **Biometric Authentication:** Relies on unique biological characteristics, such as fingerprints, retina scans, or voice recognition, to authenticate users.

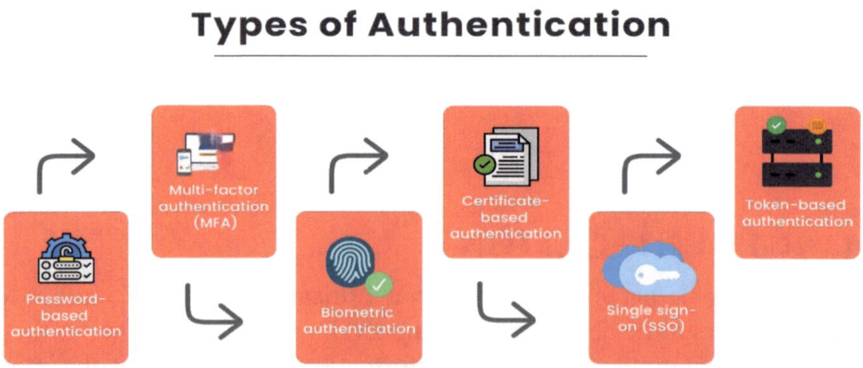

Figure 2.1. Types of authentications.

- Authentication Protocols:
  i. **Kerberos:** A widely used authentication protocol that uses tickets issued by a trusted third-party server to allow users to prove their identity (Figure 2.2).

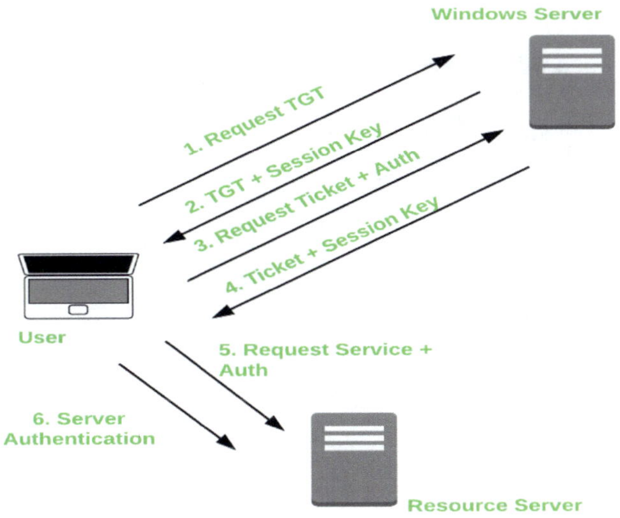

Figure 2.2. Kerberos.

  ii. **RADIUS:** A networking protocol that provides centralized Authentication, Authorization, and Accounting (AAA) management for users connecting to a network (Figure 2.3).

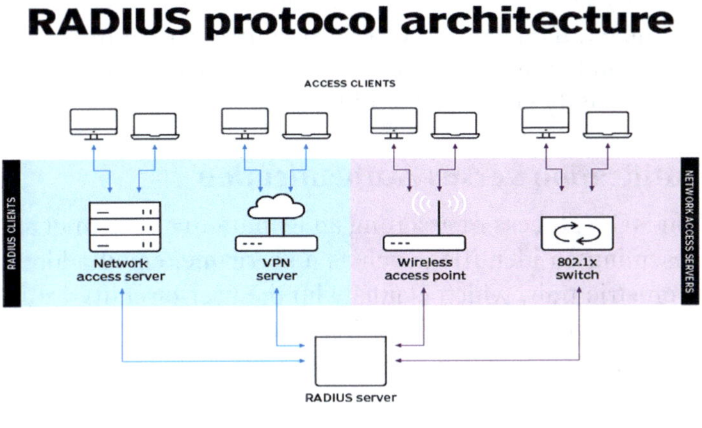

Figure 2.3. RADIUS protocol architecture.

iii. **OAuth:** Commonly used in web applications, OAuth allows third-party services to exchange tokens instead of credentials for authentication (Figure 2.4).

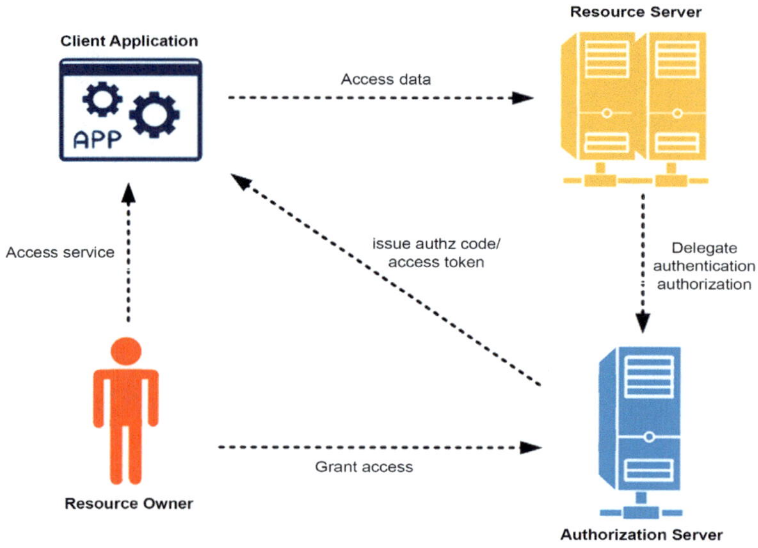

Figure 2.4. OAuth.

- Importance of Authentication in Network Security: Proper authentication mechanisms are essential to prevent unauthorized access, protect against breaches, and ensure that sensitive information is only accessible to legitimate users. As networks become more complex, the adoption of robust authentication methods, including MFA and biometric systems, is critical to maintaining security in an increasingly connected world.

2.1.1. Identification versus Authentication

Identification is the process of asserting an identity to a system or service. This involves presenting an identifier, such as a username, email address, ID card, or even a biometric trait, which claims who the user or entity is. The primary goal of identification is to establish a link between a user and their purported identity. For example, when you enter a username or swipe an ID card, you are identifying yourself to the system, signaling who you claim to be. At this stage, the system does not yet verify the truth of this claim; it only acknowledges the identity presented.

Authentication follows identification and is the process of verifying that the claimed identity is valid and belongs to the person or entity presenting it. This verification is done by requiring credentials, such as a password, PIN, security token, fingerprint, or other forms of evidence. The goal of authentication is to confirm that the person or entity attempting to access the system is genuinely who they claim to be. For example, after entering a username, you may be prompted to enter a password or provide a fingerprint scan. The system then checks these credentials against stored data to verify the user's identity.

2.1.2. Authentication Based on Phrases and Facts

Authentication based on phrases and facts is a method of identity verification that relies on personalized knowledge, such as memorable phrases or facts, unique to the individual. This approach is often considered an alternative or supplement to traditional authentication methods like passwords or biometric data, providing an additional layer of security.

- How It Works: In this method, during the enrollment process, the user selects or is assigned a set of phrases or facts that are personal and memorable. These could be responses to questions like "What was the name of your first pet?" or "What is your favorite book?" Alternatively, users might choose specific phrases that are meaningful to them but not easily guessable by others, such as a favorite quote or a sentence with a unique structure.

When the user attempts to authenticate, the system presents a challenge by asking for the correct phrase or fact. The user must provide the exact or nearly exact response that matches the stored answer. The system verifies the response, allowing access if it matches the pre-established data.

- Benefits:
  - **i. Personalization:** Because the phrases and facts are personal, they can be easier for users to remember compared to complex passwords.
  - **ii. Security:** Unlike static passwords, the specificity and uniqueness of the phrases or facts reduce the likelihood of guessing attacks or breaches through traditional methods.
  - **iii. Multi-Factor Authentication:** This method can be combined with other authentication factors (something you know, something you have, something you are) to enhance overall security.
- Limitations:

i. **Memorability vs. Security:** If the chosen facts are too simple or commonly known, security could be compromised.

ii. **Phishing Risks:** Users might inadvertently reveal these facts through social engineering attacks or phishing, potentially compromising their security.

2.1.3. Authentication Based on Biometrics

Authentication based on biometrics uses unique biological characteristics—such as fingerprints, facial recognition, iris patterns, or voice recognition—to verify a person's identity. These biometric traits are difficult to replicate or steal, providing a high level of security. When a user attempts to authenticate, the system captures their biometric data and compares it to the stored template in the system. If the data matches, access is granted.

- Benefits:

  i. **High Security:** Biometrics are unique to individuals, making them difficult to forge.

  ii. **Convenience:** No need to remember passwords or carry tokens.

- Limitations:

  i. **Privacy Concerns:** Biometric data is sensitive and, if compromised, cannot be changed like a password.

  ii. **False Positives/Negatives:** Though rare, errors in recognition can occur.

2.1.4. Authentication Based on Tokens

Authentication is a fundamental aspect of cybersecurity, ensuring that users or systems are who they claim to be before granting access to resources. One modern and increasingly popular method of authentication is token-based authentication. This approach offers several advantages, including enhanced security, scalability, and flexibility. In this overview, we'll explore the concept of token-based authentication, its types, benefits, and implementation considerations.

- **What is Token-based Authentication?:** Token-based authentication is a method where an application verifies a user's identity by issuing a token, a small piece of data, rather than relying on traditional authentication methods like passwords. After a user successfully logs in, the server generates a token that encapsulates user information and authentication details. This token is then sent to the client, which includes it in subsequent requests to authenticate itself (Figure 2.5).

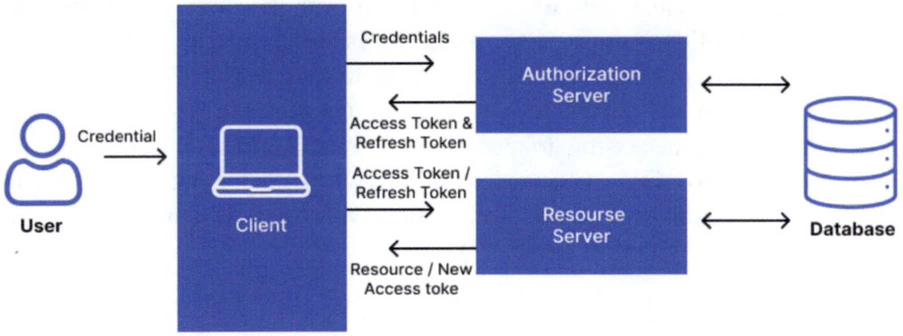

Figure 2.5. Token-based authentication.

Tokens are often used in combination with modern web technologies and are essential for managing sessions in a stateless manner. They can be employed in various contexts, including web applications, APIs, and mobile apps.

- Types of Tokens:
  i. **JSON Web Tokens (JWT):** These are a widely adopted standard for token-based authentication. They consist of three parts: a header, a payload, and a signature. The header typically specifies the token type and signing algorithm, while the payload contains the claims or user information. The signature, created using the header and payload, ensures the token's integrity and authenticity. JWTs are popular because they are compact, URL-safe, and can be easily parsed (Figure 2.6).

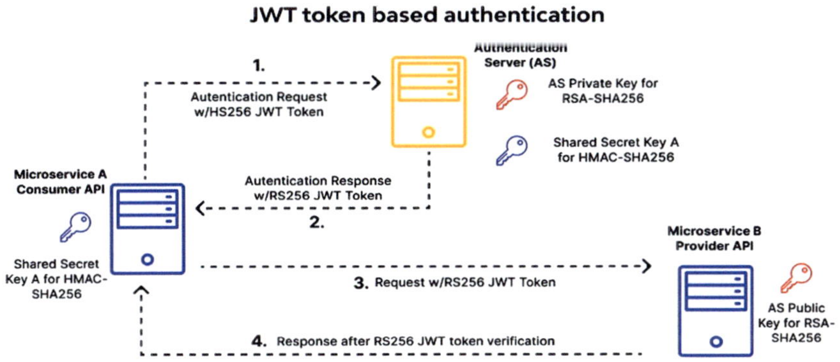

Figure 2.6. JWT token-based authentication.

ii. **OAuth Tokens:** OAuth is an authorization framework that allows third-party applications to access user data without exposing credentials. OAuth tokens are used in the context of OAuth protocols, such as OAuth 2.0. These tokens can be accessing tokens (to access resources) or refresh tokens (to obtain new access tokens). OAuth tokens are crucial for enabling secure interactions between clients and service providers (Figure 2.7).

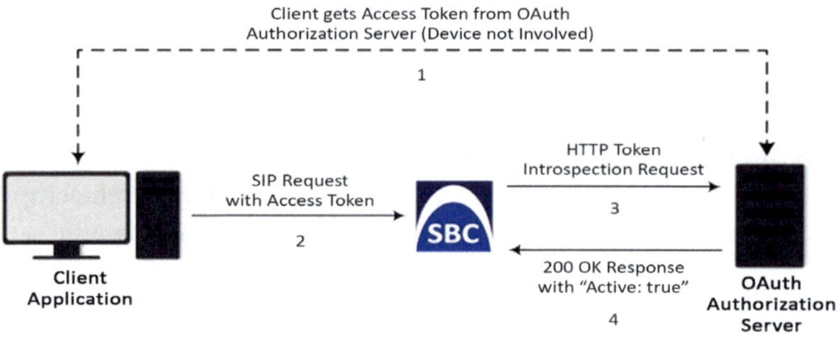

Figure 2.7. OAuth token-based authentication.

iii. **API Tokens:** These are used to authenticate and authorize access to APIs. They are often simpler than JWTs and are typically included in request headers or URL parameters. API tokens are useful for ensuring that only authorized clients can interact with an API (Figure 2.8).

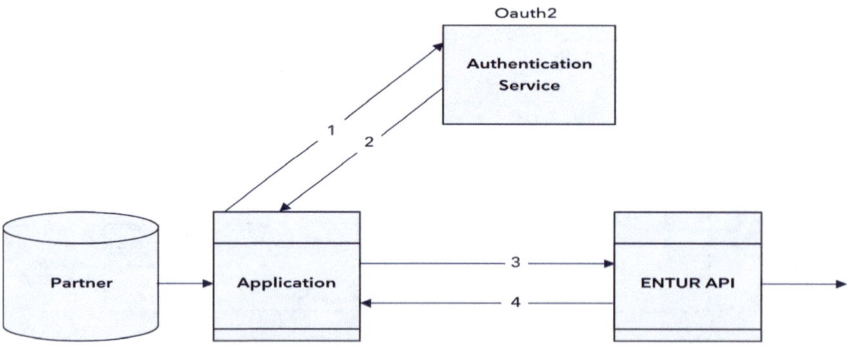

Figure 2.8. API token-based authentication.

- of Token-based Authentication:
  i. **Statelessness:** Token-based authentication is inherently stateless, meaning the server does not need to store session information. This stateless nature simplifies scaling, as any server in a cluster can process a request if it has access to the token.
  ii. **Decoupled Authentication:** Tokens can be used across different services or domains, allowing for single sign-on (SSO) and integration between disparate systems. This decoupling improves user experience and reduces the need for multiple logins.
  iii. **Enhanced Security:** Tokens can be designed to be short-lived and include information such as expiration times. This reduces the risk associated with token theft. Additionally, the use of cryptographic signatures (as in JWT) ensures that tokens cannot be tampered with without detection.
  iv. **Flexibility and Scalability:** Token-based authentication can easily be implemented in various environments, including web applications, mobile apps, and distributed systems. This flexibility supports scalability and adapts to different architectural patterns.
- Considerations:
  i. **Token Storage:** While tokens offer many advantages, secure storage on the client side is crucial. In web applications, tokens should be stored in HTTP-only cookies to mitigate the risk of cross-site scripting (XSS) attacks. For mobile applications, secure storage mechanisms provided by the operating system should be used.
  ii. **Token Expiration and Renewal:** Tokens should have a reasonable expiration time to minimize security risks. Refresh tokens can be used to obtain new access tokens without requiring the user to re-authenticate. Proper handling of token expiration and renewal is essential for maintaining a seamless user experience.
  iii. **Security Best Practices:** Implementing secure token transmission using HTTPS is vital to prevent token interception. Additionally, using strong cryptographic algorithms for token signing and validation enhances security. Regularly reviewing and updating token-related practices helps address emerging threats.

iv. **Revocation Mechanisms:** Tokens should have a mechanism for revocation in case of misuse or compromise. While tokens are stateless, maintaining a revocation list or implementing token invalidation strategies is important for ensuring security.

2.1.5. Federated Identity Management

Federated Identity Management (FIM) enables users to access multiple applications across different organizations using a single set of credentials. By establishing trust relationships between Identity Providers (IdPs) and Service Providers (SPs), FIM facilitates Single Sign-On (SSO), allowing users to log in once and access various services seamlessly. Key protocols like SAML, OAuth, and OpenID Connect ensure secure communication between these entities.

FIM enhances security by centralizing authentication, reducing the risk of password-related breaches, and lowering the administrative burden associated with managing multiple credentials. It's widely used in enterprise collaboration, B2B applications, and cloud services. However, challenges include ensuring interoperability, maintaining trust, and balancing security with user experience. Overall, FIM streamlines access while improving security across diverse platforms and applications.

2.1.6. Multi-Factor Authentication (MFA)

Multi-factor authentication (MFA) is a security approach that requires users to provide two or more verification factors to gain access to a system, application, or account. This adds an extra layer of protection beyond just a username and password. The factors typically fall into three categories (Figure 2.9):

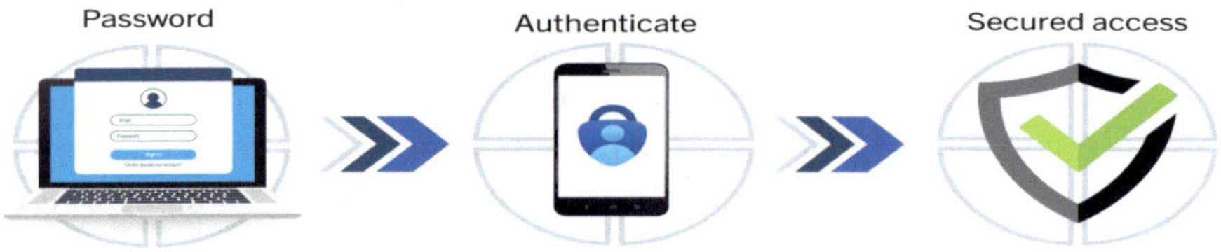

Figure 2.9. *Multi-factor authentication.*

i. **Something You Know:** This includes passwords or PINs.

ii. **Something You Have:** This refers to physical devices like smartphones, hardware tokens, or smart cards that generate time-sensitive codes.

iii. **Something You Are:** This encompasses biometric verification methods such as fingerprints, facial recognition, or voice recognition.

MFA significantly enhances security by making it more difficult for unauthorized users to gain access, even if they have compromised one factor (like a password). It is widely used in various applications, including online banking, corporate networks, and personal accounts. By requiring multiple forms of verification, MFA helps protect sensitive information and reduces the risk of identity theft and data breaches.

2.1.7. Secure Authentication

Secure authentication is the process of verifying a user's identity to ensure that only authorized individuals gain access to systems and data. It involves various methods and technologies to strengthen security, such as passwords, biometrics, and Multi-Factor Authentication (MFA).

Strong passwords combined with complexity requirements help mitigate unauthorized access. Biometric methods, like fingerprints or facial recognition, offer unique and hard-to-replicate verification. MFA enhances security by requiring multiple forms of authentication, making it difficult for attackers to breach accounts, even if they obtain one factor.

Secure authentication also encompasses best practices like regular password updates, the use of password managers, and monitoring for suspicious activity. Additionally, implementing protocols such as OAuth and SAML can facilitate secure access across platforms while maintaining user privacy. By adopting secure authentication measures, organizations can protect sensitive information and significantly reduce the risk of data breaches and identity theft.

2.2. ACCESS CONTROL

Access Control in the Centre for Internet Security (CIS) framework focuses on managing who can access specific resources within an organization. It ensures that only authorized users have the appropriate permissions to access sensitive data and systems, thereby reducing the risk of data breaches.

CIS emphasizes the principle of least privilege, granting users the minimum level of access necessary for their roles. This approach limits potential damage from compromised accounts or insider threats. The framework advocates for implementing strong authentication methods, such as Multi-Factor Authentication (MFA), and regularly reviewing user access rights.

Additionally, CIS recommends the use of role-based access control (RBAC) to streamline permissions and enhance security. Monitoring and logging access attempts are crucial for detecting unauthorized access and responding to incidents. By following CIS guidelines for access control, organizations can create a robust security posture that protects critical assets and data from unauthorized access.

2.2.1. Access Policies

Access policies are rules and guidelines that govern who can access specific resources within an organization and under what conditions. These policies are essential for protecting sensitive information and maintaining security. They define user roles, permissions, and the level of access granted based on criteria such as job function, department, or security clearance.

Effective access policies often incorporate the principle of least privilege, ensuring users receive only the access necessary to perform their duties. They can be enforced through various access control models, including Role-Based Access Control (RBAC) and Attribute-Based Access Control (ABAC).

Regularly reviewing and updating access policies is crucial to adapting to organizational changes, ensuring compliance with regulations, and mitigating risks. By establishing clear access policies, organizations can enhance their security posture, prevent unauthorized access, and ensure accountability through auditing and monitoring of access activities. This ultimately helps protect critical data and systems from potential threats.

2.2.2. Implementing Access Control

Implementing access control involves establishing a framework that governs how users interact with resources in an organization. The process begins with defining user roles and permissions based on the principle of least privilege, ensuring that individuals have only the access necessary for their responsibilities.

Next, organizations should choose an appropriate access control model, such as Role-Based Access Control (RBAC) or Attribute-Based Access Control (ABAC), to streamline the management of permissions. Strong authentication methods, including Multi-Factor Authentication (MFA), should be implemented to verify user identities before granting access.

Regular audits and reviews of access rights are essential to identify and rectify any discrepancies, ensuring compliance with policies and regulations. Additionally, organizations should establish a clear process for on boarding and off boarding users to maintain security throughout their lifecycle. By effectively implementing access control, organizations can safeguard sensitive data and resources while minimizing the risk of unauthorized access.

2.2.3. Procedure-Oriented Access Control

Procedure-Oriented Access Control focuses on defining and enforcing access rights based on established procedures and workflows within an organization. This approach emphasizes the importance of documented processes to regulate who can access specific resources and under what conditions. Access decisions are often linked to formal procedures that dictate how tasks are performed, ensuring that users adhere to predefined protocols.

In a procedure-oriented system, roles and permissions are mapped to specific tasks, which helps streamline access management. For instance, only employees involved in a particular workflow, such as document review or financial transactions, are granted the necessary permissions. This ensures that access aligns with business processes, reducing the risk of unauthorized actions.

Implementing procedure-oriented access control requires thorough documentation of workflows and regular training for employees to understand their roles. Regular audits are also essential to ensure compliance with established procedures. By prioritizing processes, this approach enhances accountability and minimizes security risks, ultimately supporting organizational goals while protecting sensitive information.

2.2.4. Role-Based Access Control

Role-Based Access Control (RBAC) is a security model that assigns permissions based on user roles within an organization. Instead of managing access at an individual level, RBAC groups users into roles that reflect their job functions, streamlining permission management. Each role is associated with specific access rights, enabling users to perform their responsibilities without unnecessary privileges.

For example, a finance department role might have access to financial systems, while an HR role would have access to employee records. This minimizes the risk of unauthorized access and adheres to the principle of least privilege.

RBAC simplifies on boarding and off boarding processes, as users can be assigned or removed from roles rather than adjusting individual permissions. Additionally, regular audits can help ensure that roles and their associated permissions remain aligned with organizational needs. Overall, RBAC enhances security and operational efficiency, making it a widely adopted approach in various industries.

2.3. CRYPTOGRAPHY

Cryptography is the practice and study of techniques for securing communication and information through the use of mathematical algorithms. Its primary goals are confidentiality, integrity, authentication, and non-repudiation. Cryptography transforms readable data (plaintext) into an unreadable format (cipher text) using encryption algorithms, ensuring that only authorized users can access the original information (Figure 2.10).

Figure 2.10. Cryptography.

There are two main types of cryptography: symmetric and asymmetric. Symmetric cryptography uses a single key for both encryption and decryption, making it efficient but requiring secure key distribution. Asymmetric cryptography, on the other hand, uses a pair of keys—one public and one private—enabling secure exchanges without the need for sharing a secret key.

Applications of cryptography include securing online communications, protecting sensitive data, and ensuring the integrity of digital signatures. As cyber threats evolve, cryptography remains a fundamental pillar of information security, safeguarding personal and organizational data against unauthorized access and tampering.

2.3.1. Problems Addressed by Encryption

Encryption addresses several critical problems in information security by transforming sensitive data into an unreadable format, ensuring that only authorized users can access it.

1. **Data Breaches:** By encrypting data at rest and in transit, organizations protect sensitive information from unauthorized access during breaches, mitigating the impact of stolen data.
2. **Confidentiality:** Encryption ensures that confidential communications, such as financial transactions or personal information, remain private, safeguarding against eavesdropping and interception.

3. **Data Integrity:** Encryption helps verify that data has not been altered during transmission, ensuring that recipients receive accurate information.
4. **Authentication:** By using encryption in digital signatures and certificates, organizations can confirm the identity of users and systems, reducing the risk of impersonation and fraud.
5. **Regulatory Compliance:** Many industries are required to encrypt sensitive data to comply with regulations like GDPR and HIPAA, helping organizations avoid legal penalties and maintain customer trust.

2.3.2. Terminology

Here are key terminologies related to access control systems (ACS):

1. **Access Control**: The mechanism that determines who can use specific resources within a system.
2. **Authentication**: The process of verifying a user's identity, typically using credentials like passwords or biometrics.
3. **Authorization**: The procedure that grants or denies access rights to authenticated users based on established policies.
4. **Role-based Access Control (RBAC)**: A model that assigns permissions based on user roles, simplifying access management.
5. **Attribute-based Access Control (ABAC)**: A more granular model that uses user, resource, and environmental attributes to determine access rights.
6. **Least Privilege**: The principle of granting users the minimum necessary access to perform their job functions.
7. **Audit Trail**: A log of access events and actions taken within the system, important for security and compliance.
8. **Access Control List (ACL)**: A list defining permissions for specific users or groups regarding resources.

2.3.3. The Data Encryption Standard (DES)

The Data Encryption Standard (DES) is a symmetric-key encryption algorithm that was widely used for securing sensitive data. Developed in the 1970s by IBM and adopted as a federal standard in 1977, DES employs a fixed 56-bit key to encrypt and decrypt data in 64-bit blocks.

DES operates through a series of complex transformations and substitutions, including initial and final permutations, as well as 16 rounds of processing that enhance security. Despite its widespread adoption, advancements in computational power led to vulnerabilities, making DES susceptible to brute-force attacks. In response to these concerns, the Advanced Encryption Standard (AES) was introduced as a more secure replacement in the early 2000s. However, DES laid the groundwork for modern encryption practices and influenced subsequent encryption algorithms. Today, while DES is largely considered obsolete, it remains an important milestone in the history of cryptography, illustrating the evolution of data security measures (Figure 2.11).

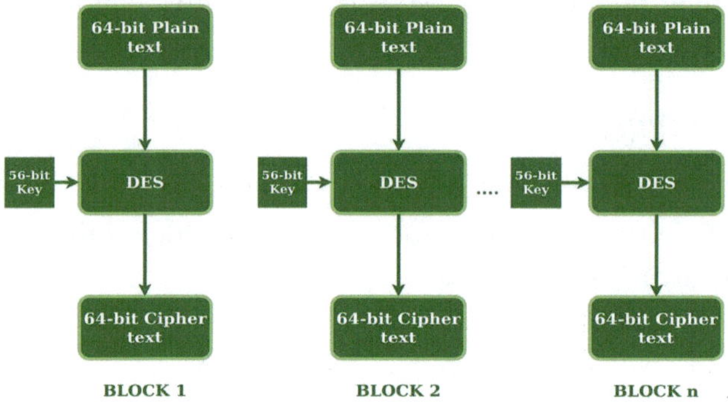

Figure 2.11. Data encryption standard.

2.3.4. Advanced Encryption System (AES)

The Advanced Encryption Standard (AES) is a symmetric-key encryption algorithm that has become the gold standard for securing sensitive data across various applications. Established by the National Institute of Standards and Technology (NIST) in 2001, AES replaced the older Data Encryption Standard (DES), which became vulnerable due to advancements in computational power and cryptanalysis techniques.

- Key Features of AES: AES operates on fixed block sizes of 128 bits and supports key lengths of 128, 192, and 256 bits. The choice of key length allows users to balance performance and security according to their specific needs. The algorithm employs a substitution-permutation network, which involves multiple rounds of processing to enhance data security. Specifically, AES typically uses 10 rounds for 128-bit keys, 12 rounds for 192-bit keys, and 14 rounds for 256-bit keys.
- How AES Works?:

  i. **Key Expansion**: The original encryption key is expanded into multiple round keys through a process involving substitution and permutation.

ii. **Initial Round**: The plaintext is combined with the first-round key using a bitwise XOR operation.

iii. **Rounds**: Each subsequent round consists of four main operations:

a. **SubBytes:** A non-linear substitution step where bytes are replaced using a fixed table (S-box).

b. **ShiftRows:** A permutation step that shifts rows of the state array cyclically.

c. **MixColumns:** A mixing operation that combines the data in each column.

d. **AddRoundKey:** The current state is combined with the round key using XOR.

iv. **Final Round:** The final round omits the MixColumns step and consists only of SubBytes, ShiftRows, and AddRoundKey.

- Applications and Impact: AES is widely adopted for securing various types of data, including communications (like SSL/TLS), file encryption, and securing wireless networks (WPA2). Its robustness and efficiency make it suitable for both software and hardware implementations, enabling its use in everything from consumer devices to enterprise-level systems.

As of today, AES remains one of the most trusted encryption standards, ensuring the confidentiality and integrity of data in an increasingly digital world, and it is a cornerstone of modern cryptographic practices (Figure 2.12).

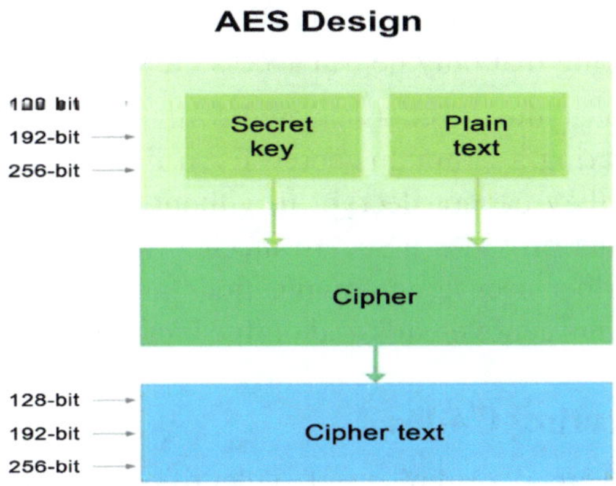

Figure 2.12. Advanced encryption system.

2.3.5. Public Key Cryptography

Public key cryptography, also known as asymmetric cryptography, is a secure communication method that utilizes a pair of keys: a public key and a private key. The public key is shared openly and can be used by anyone to encrypt messages intended for the key's owner. Conversely, the private key is kept secret and is used to decrypt messages that were encrypted with the corresponding public key.

This system enhances security by eliminating the need for both parties to share a secret key, reducing the risk of interception during key exchange. Public key cryptography also enables digital signatures, allowing users to verify the authenticity and integrity of messages, ensuring they haven't been altered during transmission.

Widely used in applications such as secure web browsing (HTTPS), email encryption, and digital certificates, public key cryptography is fundamental to modern cybersecurity, facilitating secure communications in an increasingly interconnected world.

2.3.6. Public Key Cryptography to Exchange Secret Keys

Public key cryptography facilitates secure key exchange over insecure channels by using asymmetric encryption. In this process, each party generates a pair of keys: a public key, which is shared openly, and a private key, which is kept secret.

To exchange a secret key using public key cryptography, Alice and Bob each generate their key pairs. Alice encrypts the secret key with Bob's public key and sends the encrypted message to him. Only Bob can decrypt this message using his private key, ensuring that only he can access the secret key.

This method mitigates the risks associated with traditional key exchange methods, such as sharing a common secret. Even if an attacker intercepts the encrypted message, they cannot decrypt it without Bob's private key. Public key cryptography thus provides a secure mechanism for establishing shared secrets, enabling further secure communications and transactions in various applications, including secure emails and online banking.

2.3.7. Error Detecting Codes

Error detecting codes are algorithms used to identify errors in data transmission or storage. These codes add redundant information to data, allowing the receiver to detect discrepancies caused by noise or interference during transmission.

Common types of error detecting codes include parity bits, which add a single bit to make the total number of 1s either even (even parity) or odd (odd parity). If the received data has a different parity, an error is detected.

Another widely used method is the cyclic redundancy check (CRC), which generates a fixed-size checksum from the data. The receiver recalculates the checksum and compares it to the sent value to check for errors.

While error detecting codes can identify many errors, they do not correct them; thus, they are often combined with error correcting codes (ECC) to enhance reliability. These techniques are essential in ensuring data integrity in communications, storage, and digital systems.

2.3.8. Trust

Trust in advanced computational systems refers to the confidence users have in the system's ability to operate securely, accurately, and reliably. This trust is essential for user adoption and system effectiveness, particularly in areas such as cloud computing, artificial intelligence, and data analytics.

Key factors contributing to trust include transparency, where systems provide clear insights into their processes and decision-making; accountability, ensuring that responsible parties are identifiable and can address issues; and robustness, demonstrating resilience against failures and attacks.

Security measures like encryption, access controls, and regular audits play a vital role in establishing trust by safeguarding sensitive data and ensuring compliance with regulations.

Furthermore, ethical considerations, particularly in AI systems, are crucial. Users must trust that algorithms are fair and free from bias. Building and maintaining trust in advanced computational systems requires continuous improvement and vigilance, ensuring that systems meet user expectations for security and performance.

2.3.9. Certificates: Trustable Identities and Public Keys

Certificates are digital documents that establish trustable identities and associate public keys with entities, such as individuals or organizations. Issued by trusted Certificate Authorities (CAs), these certificates verify that the public key contained within them belongs to the entity specified.

When a user receives a certificate, they can validate its authenticity by checking the CA's digital signature. This process ensures that the public key can be trusted for secure communications, such as encrypting data or verifying digital signatures.

Certificates are crucial in various applications, including secure web browsing (HTTPS), email encryption, and virtual private networks (VPNs). They help prevent man-in-the-middle attacks by assuring users that they are communicating with the intended party.

By providing a reliable framework for identity verification, certificates play a vital role in modern cybersecurity, fostering trust in online interactions and enabling secure data exchange across networks.

2.3.10. Digital Signatures – All the Pieces

Digital signatures are cryptographic tools that verify the authenticity and integrity of digital messages or documents. They rely on asymmetric encryption, using a pair of keys: a private key for signing and a public key for verification.

The process begins when the sender generates a hash of the message, creating a unique digital fingerprint. This hash is then encrypted with the sender's private key, forming the digital signature. The signed message, along with the signature, is sent to the recipient.

Upon receipt, the recipient uses the sender's public key to decrypt the signature and retrieve the hash. They then generate a hash of the received message and compare it to the decrypted hash. If they match, it confirms that the message is authentic and has not been altered.

Digital signatures enhance security in various applications, including software distribution, financial transactions, and legal documents, ensuring trust and accountability in digital communications.

CHAPTER 3

PROGRAMS AND PROGRAMMING

Contents

3.1. UNINTENTIONAL (NON-MALICIOUS) PROGRAMMING OVERSIGHTS

Unintentional programming oversights, often termed bugs, can arise from simple mistakes or misjudgments by developers, even in well-intentioned code. One common oversight is off-by-one errors, where loops iterate one time too few or too many, leading to incorrect outputs or missed conditions. For instance, when processing arrays, failing to account for zero-based indexing can result in array access errors.

Another frequent issue is incorrect data type handling. For example, treating an integer as a string can lead to unexpected results during calculations or comparisons. This type of oversight can be particularly problematic in languages with less strict type enforcement.

Logical errors also fall into this category; a programmer might assume a function is returning the correct value when it's not, leading to flawed program behavior. Additionally, misconfigured environment variables or hardcoded paths can disrupt functionality when the code is run in different environments.

These unintentional oversights, while not malicious, highlight the importance of thorough testing, code reviews, and attention to detail in programming practices to ensure reliability and correctness in software development.

3.1.1. Buffer Overflow

A buffer overflow occurs when a program writes more data to a buffer than it can hold, causing adjacent memory locations to be overwritten. This vulnerability can lead to unpredictable behavior, crashes, or security exploits, as attackers may manipulate the overflow to execute arbitrary code.

Typically, buffer overflows exploit fixed-size buffers in languages like C and C++, where memory management is manual. For instance, if a program allocates a buffer of 10 bytes but receives 15 bytes of input, the extra data can overwrite critical memory areas, such as function return addresses.

To mitigate buffer overflow risks, developers can employ safer programming practices, such as using bounds-checking functions, employing languages with automatic memory management, and implementing stack canaries. Regular code audits and utilizing tools that detect vulnerabilities during the development process also help in identifying and mitigating buffer overflow issues, ultimately enhancing software security.

3.1.2. Incomplete Mediation

Incomplete mediation refers to a security vulnerability where a system fails to properly validate input or requests before processing them, allowing unauthorized actions or access. This occurs when access controls are only enforced at one point in the application, leaving other entry points vulnerable.

For example, consider a web application that allows users to modify their account details. If access control checks are implemented only on the interface level but not in the backend logic, a malicious user might directly manipulate URLs or API endpoints to gain unauthorized access to change another user's account information. This oversight can lead to data breaches, unauthorized data manipulation, or privilege escalation.

The implications of incomplete mediation can be severe, particularly in applications handling sensitive data, such as banking or healthcare systems. Attackers can exploit these weaknesses to execute actions that should be restricted, compromising the integrity and confidentiality of the system.

To mitigate incomplete mediation vulnerabilities, developers should ensure that access controls are uniformly enforced across all entry points, including APIs, user interfaces, and backend services. Regular security audits and threat modeling can help identify potential vulnerabilities. Additionally, employing a principle of least privilege—where users are granted the minimum level of access necessary—further strengthens the system's defenses against such exploits. Ultimately, a comprehensive approach to security, encompassing thorough testing and validation, is essential to prevent incomplete mediation and enhance application security.

3.1.3. Time-of-Check to Time-of-Use

Time-of-Check to Time-of-Use (TOCTOU) is a concurrency vulnerability that occurs when a program checks a condition and then uses that information later, allowing an attacker to manipulate the system between those two events. This time window can lead to unintended actions or security breaches.

For instance, consider a scenario where a program checks if a user has permission to access a file. If an attacker exploits the gap between the permission check and the file access (e.g., by replacing the file with a symbolic link), they may gain unauthorized access to sensitive data. TOCTOU vulnerabilities are particularly relevant in multi-threaded or multi-user environments, where timing can be unpredictable. To mitigate these risks, developers should adopt atomic operations, which ensure that checks and subsequent actions are performed as a single, indivisible step. Additionally, applying strict access controls and regularly auditing code can help reduce the likelihood of TOCTOU vulnerabilities.

3.1.4. Undocumented Access Point

An undocumented access point refers to a hidden or unofficial entry method into a system or application that is not recorded in the documentation. These access points can be created intentionally or inadvertently, often during development, testing, or debugging phases.

For example, a developer might leave a backdoor for internal use, such as a hardcoded admin password or an API endpoint meant for debugging. If such access points are not secured or removed before deployment, they can be exploited by malicious actors to gain unauthorized access to sensitive data or functions.

The risks associated with undocumented access points are significant, as they can bypass established security measures. To mitigate these vulnerabilities, organizations should enforce strict code review practices, conduct thorough security audits, and implement proper access controls. Regularly testing for hidden entry points, along with maintaining comprehensive documentation, is crucial for ensuring the integrity and security of software systems.

3.1.5. Off-by-One Error

An off-by-one error is a common programming mistake where a loop or conditional statement iterates one time too few or too many times, typically due to a misunderstanding of indexing or boundaries. This type of error often occurs in languages that use zero-based indexing, such as C, C++, and Java.

For instance, consider a loop intended to process an array of ten elements. If a developer writes a loop that runs from 0 to 10, they inadvertently include an eleventh iteration, which can lead to accessing memory outside the array bounds and potentially causing crashes or unpredictable behavior. Conversely, if they mistakenly run the loop from 1 to 9, they may miss processing the first and last elements entirely.

Off-by-one errors can also arise in conditional statements. For example, a function meant to check if a number is within a specific range may incorrectly include or exclude boundary values due to an oversight in the comparison operators.

To mitigate off-by-one errors, developers should employ careful boundary checks, thorough testing, and code reviews. Utilizing tools that catch such mistakes during development can also significantly reduce their occurrence, ultimately leading to more reliable code.

3.1.6. Integer Overflow

Integer overflow occurs when an arithmetic operation attempts to exceed the maximum limit of an integer data type, causing the value to wrap around to a negative or unintended positive number. This vulnerability can lead to unexpected behavior, crashes, or security exploits in software applications.

For example, consider a scenario where a program adds two large integers, but the resulting sum exceeds the maximum value representable by that integer type (e.g., 32-bit signed integers have a maximum value of 2,147,483,647). If the operation does not properly check for overflow, the result may wrap around to a negative value, potentially leading to erroneous logic or triggering security vulnerabilities.

Attackers can exploit integer overflow by deliberately crafting inputs that cause overflow conditions, which may allow them to manipulate program flow, bypass security checks, or corrupt memory. This exploitation is particularly concerning in critical systems like banking or medical applications, where precision and correctness are paramount.

To mitigate the risks associated with integer overflow, developers can use larger data types (such as 64-bit integers), implement bounds-checking to validate arithmetic operations, and utilize programming languages or libraries that automatically handle overflow conditions. Additionally, conducting thorough testing, including fuzz testing and static analysis, can help identify potential overflow vulnerabilities, enhancing overall software security and reliability.

3.1.7. Unterminated Null-Terminated String

An unterminated null-terminated string is a common programming error that occurs when a string is not properly terminated with a null character (\0). In languages like C and C++, strings are represented as arrays of characters, with the null character indicating the end of the string. When a string lacks this terminator, functions that rely on it to determine the string's length can lead to undefined behavior.

For example, if a developer initializes a character array but forgets to add the null terminator, functions such as strlen or printf may continue reading beyond the intended memory space, leading to memory corruption, crashes, or exposure of sensitive data. This vulnerability can also open doors for security exploits, as attackers might manipulate input to read or modify adjacent memory.

To mitigate risks associated with unterminated strings, developers should ensure that every string is properly terminated when created or manipulated. Using safer string handling functions, like snprintf instead of sprintf, can help prevent overflow and ensure proper termination. Additionally, incorporating static analysis tools can assist in identifying potential issues during development. Regular code reviews and adhering to best practices in memory management further enhance robustness and security, reducing the likelihood of errors associated with null-terminated strings.

3.1.8. Parameter Length, Type, and Number

Parameter length, type, and number are critical aspects of function and method design in programming that significantly impact both functionality and security. Ensuring that parameters are correctly defined and validated can help prevent various vulnerabilities and bugs.

- Length: This refers to the size or number of characters that an input parameter can accept. Setting proper length constraints is essential to prevent buffer overflow attacks, where an attacker inputs excessively long data to manipulate program behavior or corrupt memory. For instance, if a function is designed to accept a username with a maximum of 30 characters, failing to enforce this limit could allow an attacker to input a longer string, causing unintended overwrites in memory.
- Type: This defines the kind of data a function expects (e.g., integer, string, float). Mismatched types can lead to logical errors or runtime crashes. For example, passing a string to a function expecting an integer can produce unexpected results or errors. Type validation is crucial for maintaining the integrity of the program and ensuring that functions behave as intended.
- Number: This refers to how many arguments a function accepts. Functions that take an excessive number of parameters can become unwieldy, making code difficult to read and maintain. Additionally, failing to validate the number of parameters can lead to unexpected behavior, such as when a function receives more arguments than it can handle.

To mitigate risks associated with parameter length, type, and number, developers should implement rigorous input validation, utilize type-safe programming languages, and maintain clear documentation. Adopting design patterns, such as using data structures or objects to encapsulate multiple related parameters, can also enhance code clarity and reduce errors. Regular code reviews and testing further ensure that functions behave correctly under various input scenarios, ultimately improving software reliability and security.

3.1.9. Unsafe Utility Program

An unsafe utility program is software designed to perform tasks that may inadvertently expose systems to vulnerabilities or security risks. These programs often lack proper input validation, error handling, or access controls, leading to potential exploits by malicious users.

For example, a file management utility that allows users to delete files without confirming the action could be dangerous. An attacker might exploit this by tricking a user into running the utility, leading to the unintentional deletion of critical system files or sensitive data.

Another example is a network scanning tool that does not restrict the range of IP addresses it can scan. If misused, this tool could be employed to target networks without authorization, violating privacy and security policies.

To mitigate risks associated with unsafe utility programs, developers should prioritize secure coding practices, including thorough input validation, implementing proper authentication mechanisms, and ensuring that actions requiring elevated privileges are well-guarded. Regular security audits and user training can also help minimize the likelihood of abuse, ensuring that utility programs are both effective and secure. Ultimately, a focus on security throughout the development lifecycle is essential to create safe and reliable utility software.

3.1.10. Race Condition

A race condition occurs in concurrent programming when the outcome of a process depends on the relative timing of events, such as the order in which threads or processes execute. This can lead to unpredictable behavior and vulnerabilities, particularly in multi-threaded applications.

For instance, consider two threads attempting to update a shared variable simultaneously without proper synchronization. If one thread reads the variable while the other is in the process of updating it, the first thread may operate on stale or incorrect data, leading to inconsistent results. This can manifest in various ways, such as lost updates, incorrect calculations, or even system crashes.

Race conditions are especially critical in security contexts. An attacker might exploit a race condition to manipulate the timing of operations, gaining unauthorized access or altering data unexpectedly.

To mitigate race conditions, developers should use synchronization mechanisms like mutexes, semaphores, or locks to ensure that only one thread can access shared resources at a time. Employing proper design patterns, such as message passing or immutability, can also help reduce the likelihood of race conditions. Thorough testing, including stress testing and code reviews, is essential for identifying and addressing these issues in concurrent applications.

3.2. MALICIOUS CODE – MALWARE

Malicious code, commonly referred to as malware, is software specifically designed to harm, exploit, or otherwise compromise computer systems, networks, or devices. Malware encompasses a variety of threats, including viruses, worms, trojans, ransomware, spyware, and adware, each with distinct behaviors and objectives. Viruses attach themselves to legitimate programs and replicate when the infected program is executed. Worms, on the other hand, spread independently across networks without needing a host file, often consuming bandwidth and resources. Trojans disguise themselves as legitimate software but carry harmful payloads that can steal data or create backdoors for attackers.

Ransomware is particularly notorious, encrypting users' files and demanding a ransom for their release, often causing significant financial and operational damage. Spyware secretly monitors user activities, collecting sensitive information like passwords and credit card numbers, while adware displays unwanted advertisements, often degrading user experience.

Malware can infiltrate systems through various vectors, including malicious email attachments, compromised websites, or software downloads. Once inside, it can execute actions ranging from data theft to system disruption.

To combat malware, individuals and organizations should employ robust cybersecurity measures, such as antivirus software, firewalls, and regular system updates. User education is crucial, as many attacks exploit human behavior, such as clicking on suspicious links or downloading unverified software. By adopting a multi-layered security approach, users can significantly reduce their risk of malware infection and protect their sensitive information from malicious actors.

3.2.1. Malware – Viruses, Trojan Horses, and Worms

Malware, short for malicious software, is a broad term that encompasses various types of harmful software designed to infiltrate, damage, or exploit computer systems. Among the most notorious categories of malware are viruses, trojan horses, and worms. Each type has unique characteristics and methods of propagation, making them essential to understand for effective cybersecurity.

- : A computer virus is a type of malware that attaches itself to legitimate programs or files. When an infected program is executed, the virus activates and replicates, often spreading to other programs and files on the system. Viruses typically require user interaction to spread; for instance, a user might unknowingly download an infected file or open a malicious email attachment.

Viruses can be particularly destructive, leading to data corruption, system slowdowns, and even total system failures. They often have payloads designed to perform malicious activities, such as deleting files or stealing sensitive information. Common examples of viruses include the ILOVEYOU virus and the Melissa virus, which spread rapidly through email and caused widespread damage.

- Trojan Horses: Or trojans, are malware that masquerade as legitimate software to trick users into installing them. Unlike viruses, trojans do not self-replicate but rely on social engineering to entice users. For example, a trojan might present itself as a game, utility, or software update. Once installed, it can perform various malicious activities, including stealing passwords, creating backdoors for remote access, or downloading additional malware.

Trojans can be particularly insidious because they often operate quietly in the background, making them difficult to detect. Examples include the Zeus trojan, which targets financial information, and the Emotet trojan, known for its ability to deliver other types of malwares.

- Worms: These are a distinct type of malware that can spread independently across networks without needing a host file. Unlike viruses, which rely on user action, worms exploit vulnerabilities in network protocols to propagate. This makes them particularly dangerous, as they can spread rapidly and infect a large number of systems in a short period.

Worms can consume significant bandwidth and resources, causing system slowdowns or crashes. One of the most famous examples of a worm is the Conficker worm, which infected millions of computers worldwide by exploiting vulnerabilities in the Windows operating system. Another notable worm is the WannaCry ransomware worm, which not only spread quickly but also encrypted user files and demanded ransom payments.

- Mitigation and Prevention: To protect against these types of malwares, users and organizations should adopt a multi-layered security strategy. This includes:

  i. **Antivirus Software:** Regularly updated antivirus programs can detect and remove known viruses, trojans, and worms.

  ii. **Firewalls:** These can help block unauthorized access to networks and systems, reducing the risk of infection.

  iii. **Regular Updates:** Keeping operating systems and software updated ensures that vulnerabilities are patched, reducing the risk of exploitation by worms and other malware.

  iv. **User Education:** Training users to recognize phishing attempts and suspicious downloads can significantly reduce the likelihood of malware infections.

  v. **Backup Data:** Regularly backing up data can mitigate the damage caused by ransomware and other destructive malware.

Understanding the differences between viruses, trojan horses, and worms is crucial for implementing effective security measures. By remaining vigilant and adopting best practices, individuals and organizations can protect themselves against the ever-evolving threat of malware.

3.2.2. Technical Details: Malicious Code

Malicious code, commonly known as malware, encompasses various types of software designed to disrupt, damage, or gain unauthorized access to computer systems. Understanding the technical details of malware is crucial for developing effective defenses against these threats. This overview covers the types of malwares, their methods of propagation, techniques used for exploitation, and potential impacts on systems.

- Types of Malwares:
  i. **Viruses:** A virus attaches itself to legitimate programs or files. It replicates when the host program is executed, spreading to other files and systems. Viruses typically require user interaction to propagate.
  ii. **Worms:** Unlike viruses, worms can self-replicate and spread autonomously across networks. They exploit vulnerabilities in operating systems or applications to propagate, often consuming bandwidth and resources.
  iii. **Trojans:** This disguise themselves as legitimate software to trick users into installation. Once installed, they can perform various malicious activities, such as data theft or opening backdoors for attackers.
  iv. **Ransomware:** This type of malware encrypts a user's files and demands a ransom for their release. Ransomware can spread via phishing emails, malicious downloads, or exploit kits.
  v. **Spyware:** These secretly monitors user activities, capturing sensitive information like passwords and credit card numbers without the user's knowledge.
- Methods: Malware can spread through various vectors:
  i. **Email Attachments**: Many malware types are delivered as attachments in phishing emails, tricking users into opening them.
  ii. **Malicious Downloads**: Users may inadvertently download malware from compromised websites or malicious software bundles.
  iii. **Exploiting Vulnerabilities**: Worms often exploit unpatched vulnerabilities in software or operating systems to spread automatically.

iv. **Social Engineering**: Malware may rely on user manipulation, encouraging them to execute harmful code.

- Techniques for Exploitation: Malware employs several techniques to evade detection and achieve its goals:

i. **Polymorphism**: This technique involves altering the code's appearance while keeping its functionality intact. By changing its structure, polymorphic malware can evade signature-based detection methods.

ii. **Rootkits**: A rootkit is a collection of tools that allow an attacker to maintain unauthorized access while hiding their presence. It modifies the operating system to conceal files, processes, or network connections related to the malware.

iii. **Keyloggers**: These tools record keystrokes to capture sensitive information, such as passwords and credit card numbers. They can be implemented as standalone software or embedded in other types of malwares.

iv. **Command and Control (C2)**: Many malware types communicate with a C2 server to receive instructions, updates, or to exfiltrate stolen data. This infrastructure allows attackers to maintain control over compromised systems.

- Impacts on Systems: The consequences of malware infections can be severe, including:

i. **Data Loss**: Malware can corrupt or delete critical data, leading to significant operational disruptions.

ii. **Financial Loss**: Ransomware attacks can result in direct financial losses, while data breaches can incur costs related to recovery, fines, and reputational damage.

iii. **System Downtime**: Infected systems may become unusable, leading to loss of productivity and increased operational costs.

iv. **Unauthorized Access**: Malware can create backdoors, allowing attackers to gain long-term access to systems for further exploitation.

Understanding the technical details of malicious code is essential for effective cybersecurity measures. By recognizing the types of malwares, their propagation methods, and exploitation techniques, individuals and organizations can implement stronger defenses. This includes using updated antivirus software, conducting regular security audits, and fostering a culture of cybersecurity awareness. Through proactive measures, the risks associated with malware can be significantly reduced, protecting both individual and organizational assets.

3.3. COUNTERMEASURES

Countermeasures against malware are essential for safeguarding systems and data from malicious attacks. Here are some effective strategies:

1. Antivirus and Anti-Malware Software: Deploy robust antivirus and anti-malware solutions that provide real-time protection and regular updates. These tools can detect, quarantine, and remove known threats before they cause harm.
2. Regular Software Updates: Keep operating systems, applications, and security software up to date to protect against vulnerabilities that malware can exploit. Enable automatic updates where possible to ensure timely patching.
3. Firewalls: Utilize both hardware and software firewalls to monitor incoming and outgoing traffic. Firewalls can block unauthorized access and prevent malicious data from entering the network.
4. User Education: Educate users about the dangers of phishing emails, suspicious downloads, and unsafe browsing practices. Training programs can help users recognize and avoid potential threats.
5. Data Backups: Regularly backup critical data to secure locations. This ensures that in the event of a ransomware attack or data corruption, vital information can be restored without paying a ransom.
6. Access Controls: Implement strict access controls, including the principle of least privilege, to limit user permissions. This minimizes the risk of malware spreading through accounts with elevated access.
7. Network Segmentation: Divide networks into smaller, isolated segments to contain potential malware outbreaks. This strategy limits the movement of malware within an organization.

By combining these countermeasures, organizations can significantly enhance their resilience against malware attacks and protect their critical assets.

3.3.1. Countermeasures for Users

Countermeasures for users are essential for maintaining personal cybersecurity and protecting sensitive information from malware and other threats. Implementing these practices can significantly reduce the risk of infection and data breaches.

1. Use Strong, Unique Passwords: Creating strong, unique passwords for each account is fundamental to security. A strong password typically includes a mix of upper- and lower-case letters, numbers, and special characters. Consider using a password manager to generate and store complex passwords securely, making it easier to maintain different passwords across multiple sites.
2. Enable Two-Factor Authentication (2FA): Two-factor authentication adds an extra layer of security by requiring a second form of verification, such as a text message or authentication app code, in addition to your password. This can significantly reduce the likelihood of unauthorized access, even if your password is compromised.
3. Regular Software Updates: Always keep your operating system, applications, and security software up to date. Software developers frequently release updates that patch security vulnerabilities, making it harder for malware to exploit known weaknesses. Enable automatic updates where possible to ensure you receive the latest protections.
4. Install and Maintain Antivirus Software: Use reputable antivirus and anti-malware software to provide real-time protection against malicious threats. Regularly update your antivirus software to ensure it can detect the latest threats. Perform routine system scans to identify and remove any hidden malware.
5. Be Cautious with Email Attachments and Links: Phishing attacks often come via email, where attackers trick users into clicking malicious links or opening infected attachments. Always verify the sender's identity and be skeptical of unexpected emails, especially those asking for sensitive information or urging immediate action. Hover over links to see the actual URL before clicking.
6. Browse Safely: Practice safe browsing habits. Avoid visiting untrusted websites or clicking on suspicious advertisements. Use browser extensions that block ads and trackers, enhancing your browsing experience and security. Consider using a virtual private network (VPN) to encrypt your internet connection, especially when using public Wi-Fi.
7. Regular Data Backups: Regularly backup your important data to an external hard drive or cloud storage. This ensures that in the event of a ransomware attack or data loss, you can restore your files without losing critical information. Automate backups, if possible, to ensure consistency.

8. Limit Personal Information Sharing: Be mindful of the personal information you share online, whether on social media or other platforms. Adjust privacy settings to limit who can see your information. Cybercriminals can use publicly available data for social engineering attacks.
9. Monitor Financial Accounts: Regularly check your bank and credit card statements for unauthorized transactions. Set up alerts for significant transactions, enabling you to act quickly in case of suspicious activity. Consider using credit monitoring services that alert you to changes in your credit report.
10. Educate Yourself about Threats: Stay informed about the latest cybersecurity threats and trends. Understanding how malware works and the methods cybercriminals use can help you recognize potential risks and avoid falling victim to attacks.

3.3.2. Countermeasures for Developers

Countermeasures for developers are essential to create secure software and protect applications from malicious threats. Implementing best practices during the development lifecycle can significantly reduce vulnerabilities. Here are key countermeasures:

1. Input Validation: Always validate and sanitize user inputs to prevent injection attacks (like SQL injection or cross-site scripting). Use whitelisting techniques to ensure that only acceptable data types and formats are processed.
2. Secure Coding Practices: Follow secure coding guidelines, such as those provided by the OWASP Foundation. Familiarize yourself with common vulnerabilities (e.g., buffer overflows, race conditions) and how to avoid them. Regularly review and refactor code for security improvements.
3. Authentication and Authorization: Implement robust authentication mechanisms, such as multi-factor authentication (MFA). Use established frameworks for authorization to ensure users have appropriate access levels. Apply the principle of least privilege to limit access to sensitive data.
4. Data Encryption: Encrypt sensitive data both in transit and at rest using strong encryption algorithms. This protects data from unauthorized access and ensures that even if data is intercepted, it remains unreadable.

5. Regular Security Testing: Incorporate security testing into your development process, including static code analysis, dynamic application testing, and penetration testing. Regularly assess your application for vulnerabilities and address any findings promptly.
6. Logging and Monitoring: Implement logging to track application activity and potential security incidents. Use monitoring tools to detect anomalies in real-time, enabling rapid responses to potential threats.
7. Update Dependencies: Regularly update libraries and frameworks to mitigate vulnerabilities associated with third-party components. Use tools that check for outdated or insecure dependencies.

3.3.3. Countermeasure Specifically for Security

Countermeasures specifically aimed at enhancing security are crucial for safeguarding systems, applications, and data from malicious threats. Here are several effective strategies:

1. Access Control Mechanisms: Implement robust access control measures to ensure that only authorized users can access sensitive information. Use role-based access control (RBAC) to assign permissions based on user roles, limiting access to what is necessary for job functions.
2. Encryption: Utilize encryption for both data at rest and data in transit. Employ strong encryption algorithms to protect sensitive data from unauthorized access. For example, using TLS for web traffic ensures that data transmitted between clients and servers is secure.
3. Regular Security Audits: Conduct regular security audits and vulnerability assessments to identify weaknesses in your systems. This includes reviewing configurations, user permissions, and security policies. Address any vulnerabilities discovered during these audits promptly.
4. Intrusion Detection and Prevention Systems (IDPS): Deploy IDPS to monitor network traffic for suspicious activities and potential threats. These systems can alert administrators to unauthorized access attempts and, in some cases, automatically block malicious traffic.
5. Security Awareness Training: Provide ongoing security awareness training for employees to educate them about common threats such as phishing, social engineering, and malware. A well-informed workforce is critical for preventing security breaches.

6. Patch Management: Implement a rigorous patch management process to ensure that all software, including operating systems and applications, is up to date with the latest security patches. This helps protect against known vulnerabilities that attackers may exploit.
7. Incident Response Plan: Develop and maintain an incident response plan that outlines procedures for detecting, responding to, and recovering from security incidents. Regularly test and update this plan to ensure its effectiveness in real scenarios.

3.3.4. Countermeasures That Don't Work

While many security countermeasures can be effective, some commonly used strategies do not provide the expected level of protection. Understanding these ineffective measures is crucial for improving security posture. Here are several countermeasures that often fall short:

1. Over Reliance on Antivirus Software: Many users believe that antivirus software alone can fully protect their systems. While antivirus solutions can detect known threats, they often fail to catch new or sophisticated malware, particularly zero-day exploits. Relying solely on antivirus can lead to a false sense of security.
2. Using Weak Passwords: Despite widespread awareness, many individuals and organizations still use weak or easily guessable passwords. Simple passwords can be easily cracked through brute force attacks or social engineering, rendering password policies ineffective.
3. Neglecting Software Updates: Failing to regularly update software and systems is a common pitfall. Many users disable automatic updates, leaving systems vulnerable to known exploits. Attackers often target outdated software that has unpatched vulnerabilities.
4. Ignoring User Education: While training employees on security best practices is essential, ineffective training sessions can lead to apathy or disengagement. If users don't see the relevance or if training is not ongoing, they may not retain critical information, increasing vulnerability.
5. Excessive Trust in Firewalls: While firewalls are essential for network security, they are not foolproof. Many users mistakenly believe that firewalls alone can protect against all threats, ignoring the need for additional layers of security such as intrusion detection systems and regular monitoring.

6. Password Managers as a Sole Solution: While password managers can enhance password security, relying solely on them without additional measures (like 2FA) can be risky. If a password manager is compromised, all stored passwords are at risk.

CHAPTER 4

THE WEB—USER SIDE

Contents

4.1. BROWSER ATTACKS

Browser attacks exploit vulnerabilities in web browsers or their extensions to compromise user security and privacy. Common types of browser attacks include:

1. **Phishing:** Attackers create fake websites that mimic legitimate ones to steal login credentials and personal information. Users are often tricked into entering sensitive data.

2. **Malware Injection:** Malicious scripts can be injected into websites, which execute when a user visits the site. This can lead to unauthorized access to the user's system, data theft, or ransomware attacks.
3. **Cross-Site Scripting (XSS):** This technique involves injecting malicious scripts into trusted websites. When users visit the affected site, the script executes in their browser, allowing attackers to steal cookies or session tokens.
4. **Drive-by Downloads:** Unsuspecting users can unknowingly download malware simply by visiting a compromised website. This often occurs without any user interaction.
5. **Man-in-the-Middle (MitM) Attacks:** In this scenario, attackers intercept communication between the user and a website, potentially capturing sensitive information. This can occur over unsecured Wi-Fi networks.

To protect against browser attacks, users should keep their browsers updated, use strong passwords, enable security features like pop-up blockers, and be cautious about clicking on links or downloading files from untrusted sources. Additionally, employing browser extensions that enhance security can provide an extra layer of protection against these threats.

4.1.1. Browser Attack Types

Browser attacks encompass various tactics targeting web browser vulnerabilities. Here are key types:

i. **Phishing:** Attackers create fake websites that mimic legitimate ones to steal sensitive information like passwords and credit card numbers.

ii. **Malware Injection:** Malicious scripts are injected into websites, executing when users visit and potentially leading to data theft or system compromise.

iii. **Cross-Site Scripting (XSS):** This attack injects harmful scripts into trusted sites, enabling attackers to steal session tokens or cookies from users.

iv. **Drive-by Downloads:** Users unknowingly download malware just by visiting a compromised site, often without any action required.

v. **Man-in-the-Middle (MitM):** Attackers intercept communication between users and websites, capturing sensitive information over unsecured networks.

To protect against these threats, users should keep browsers updated, use strong, unique passwords, and be cautious of suspicious links and downloads.

4.1.2. How Browser Attacks Succeed: Failed Identification and Authentication

Browser attacks often succeed due to failures in identification and authentication processes, which can leave users vulnerable to a range of cyber threats. Here's a deeper look at how these failures contribute to the success of browser attacks.

- Weak Password Practices: One of the primary causes of successful browser attacks is the use of weak or reused passwords. Many users rely on easily memorable passwords or use the same password across multiple sites. This practice makes it easy for attackers to compromise accounts, especially if they employ credential stuffing techniques, where stolen credentials from one breach are used to access accounts on other platforms. When users fail to adopt strong, unique passwords, they inadvertently create openings for attackers.
- Phishing Techniques: Phishing remains one of the most effective methods for breaching authentication. Attackers often craft convincing emails or messages that lead users to fraudulent websites resembling legitimate ones. When users enter their credentials on these sites, attackers capture their login information. Poor user awareness about identifying phishing attempts contributes significantly to this vulnerability. Without proper training or awareness, users may not recognize suspicious URLs or email addresses.

4.2. WEB ATTACKS TARGETING USERS

Web attacks targeting users exploit various vulnerabilities to steal sensitive information or compromise systems. Here are some prevalent types:

1. Phishing: It is one of the most common web attacks. Attackers send deceptive emails or messages that lead users to fake websites resembling legitimate ones. Once users enter their login credentials or personal information, attackers capture this data for malicious use.
2. Malware: This can be delivered through malicious websites or downloads. Users may unknowingly download malware by clicking on harmful links or ads. This malware can steal data, monitor user activities, or encrypt files for ransom.

3. Cross-Site Scripting (XSS): In XSS attacks, attackers inject malicious scripts into trusted websites. When users interact with these sites, the scripts execute in their browsers, allowing attackers to steal cookies, session tokens, or sensitive data.
4. Drive-by Downloads: This attack occurs when users visit a compromised website, leading to automatic downloads of malware without their consent. Users might not even be aware that they have been infected.
5. Man-in-the-Middle (MitM) Attacks: In MitM attacks, attackers intercept communication between users and websites. This can happen over unsecured networks, allowing attackers to capture login details and other sensitive information.
6. Credential Stuffing: Attackers use stolen usernames and passwords from one service to gain access to accounts on other platforms, exploiting users' tendency to reuse credentials.

4.2.1. False or Misleading Content

False or misleading content has become a pervasive issue in today's digital landscape, affecting individuals, organizations, and societies at large. This type of content can take various forms, including misinformation, disinformation, and malinformation.

- Misinformation: These refers to false or misleading information shared without harmful intent. It often spreads through social media, news articles, or word of mouth, as individuals share content, they believe to be true. For example, viral posts about health remedies may lack scientific backing, leading to public confusion and potentially harmful behaviors.
- Disinformation: It is deliberately false information spread with the intent to deceive. This is often seen in political contexts, where fabricated news stories or manipulated images aim to influence public opinion or sway elections. Such tactics can undermine trust in institutions and erode democratic processes.
- Malinformation: This involves sharing genuine information with the intent to cause harm, often by taking it out of context. This can include exposing private information or selectively presenting facts to mislead the audience. For instance, disclosing sensitive personal data can lead to harassment or identity theft.
- Consequences: The spread of false or misleading content can have

serious consequences, including public panic, decreased trust in media and institutions, and the polarization of communities. It can also impede informed decision-making, particularly in critical areas like health, politics, and environmental issues.

- Combating False Content: Addressing this challenge requires media literacy, critical thinking, and responsible sharing practices. Users should verify information through reputable sources, be wary of sensational headlines, and understand the motivations behind the content they encounter. Platforms also play a crucial role by implementing policies to flag or remove misleading content, fostering a more informed public discourse.

4.2.2. Malicious Web Content

Malicious web content refers to harmful material intentionally designed to exploit vulnerabilities in users' systems or deceive them into compromising their security. This content can take various forms and poses significant risks to individuals and organizations alike.

- Types of Malicious Web Content:
  - **i. Malware:** This includes software designed to harm or exploit devices, such as viruses, worms, and ransomware. Malware can be delivered via malicious links, downloads, or compromised websites, often without the user's knowledge.
  - **ii. Phishing Sites:** These fraudulent websites mimic legitimate ones to trick users into providing sensitive information, like login credentials or credit card details. Phishing attacks can occur through deceptive emails or fake social media profiles.
  - **iii. Drive-by Downloads:** This method automatically downloads malicious software when a user visits an infected website. Users may not even realize they've downloaded anything until it's too late, leading to potential system compromise.
  - **iv. Ad Fraud:** Malicious ads can redirect users to harmful sites or download malware without their consent. These ads often appear on legitimate websites, making them hard to identify.
  - **v. Exploit Kits:** These are tools that automate the process of exploiting known vulnerabilities in software. When users visit a compromised site, the exploit kit can deploy malware to their devices based on detected vulnerabilities.
- Consequences and Prevention: The impact of malicious web content can be severe, resulting in data breaches, financial loss, and identity

theft. To mitigate these risks, users should adopt proactive measures, such as:

- Keeping software and browsers up to date;
- Using reputable antivirus and anti-malware solutions;
- Being cautious of unknown links or downloads;
- Employing browser extensions that block malicious content.

4.2.3. Protecting Against Malicious Web Pages

Protecting against malicious web pages is essential for maintaining online security and safeguarding personal and sensitive information. As cyber threats become increasingly sophisticated, users must adopt proactive measures to mitigate risks. Here's a comprehensive guide on how to protect against these dangers.

- Understanding Malicious Web Pages: Malicious web pages are designed to harm users or their devices. They can host malware, facilitate phishing attacks, or exploit vulnerabilities in software. These pages may appear legitimate, making it challenging for users to identify them as threats. Common tactics include deceptive URLs, social engineering, and drive-by downloads.
- Strategies for Protection:
  - i. **Keep Software Updated:** Regularly update your operating system, web browsers, and any installed applications. Software updates often include security patches that fix vulnerabilities exploited by attackers.
  - ii. **Use Reliable Security Software:** Install reputable antivirus and anti-malware software. These tools can help detect and block malicious web pages before they cause harm. Regularly update these programs to ensure optimal protection.
  - iii. **Enable Browser Security Features:** Modern browsers come equipped with security features that help identify and block harmful sites. Enable options like pop-up blockers, phishing protection, and safe browsing modes. Familiarize yourself with your browser's security settings and customize them for enhanced safety.
  - iv. **Be Cautious with Links:** Avoid clicking on links from unknown sources, especially in emails or social media messages. Hover over links to reveal their true URLs before clicking. If a link seems suspicious, it's better to navigate to

the website directly through a search engine.

v. **Utilize a Virtual Private Network (VPN):** A VPN encrypts your internet connection, providing an additional layer of security, especially when using public Wi-Fi. This can help prevent man-in-the-middle attacks, where attackers intercept your data.

vi. **Implement Multi-Factor Authentication (MFA):** Enabling MFA adds an extra layer of security to your online accounts. Even if a malicious web page manages to capture your credentials, MFA can prevent unauthorized access.

vii. **Educate Yourself on Phishing Techniques:** Familiarize yourself with common phishing tactics, such as urgency cues, grammatical errors, and unfamiliar sender addresses. Awareness is your first line of defense against deceptive emails and messages.

viii. **Use a Password Manager:** A password manager can help create and store strong, unique passwords for each of your accounts. This reduces the risk of credential stuffing attacks, where attackers use stolen passwords from one site to gain access to others.

ix. **Regularly Back Up Data:** Regularly backup important files to an external hard drive or a secure cloud service. In the event of a malware attack or data loss, having backups can mitigate the damage.

x. **Report Suspicious Activity:** If you encounter a suspicious web page, report it to your browser's security team or a dedicated anti-phishing organization. This helps others avoid potential threats and strengthens overall online security.

4.3. OBTAINING USER OR WEBSITE DATA

Obtaining user or website data involves various techniques and methods, both legitimate and malicious. Here's an overview:

- Legitimate Methods:

i. **User Consent:** Websites often collect data through user consent mechanisms, such as registration forms, surveys, or cookie notifications. Users willingly provide information in exchange for services or personalized experiences.

ii. **Analytics Tools:** Websites use tools like Google Analytics to gather data on user behavior, including page views, session duration, and demographics. This helps site owners optimize user experience and marketing strategies.

iii. **APIs:** Many platforms offer APIs (Application Programming Interfaces) that allow developers to access specific data. This enables third-party applications to retrieve user or website data in a structured manner, often with user consent.

- Malicious Methods:

i. **Phishing:** Attackers create fake websites or emails to deceive users into providing sensitive information, such as passwords or credit card details.

ii. **Web Scraping:** This technique involves automated bots that extract data from websites without permission. While some sites permit scraping, others may consider it a violation of their terms of service.

iii. **Exploiting Vulnerabilities:** Cybercriminals may exploit security flaws in a website's code to access databases containing user information.

4.3.1. Code Within Data Website Data: A User's Problem, Too Foiling Data Attacks

In the digital age, where data is considered the new oil, securing website data has become a paramount concern for both organizations and users. Data breaches, malware attacks, and unauthorized access can lead to significant financial loss, identity theft, and erosion of trust. While companies must implement robust security measures, users also play a critical role in foiling data attacks.

- Understanding the Threat Landscape: Cybercriminals are constantly evolving their tactics to exploit vulnerabilities in websites and user behavior. Common methods include:

i. SQL Injection: Attackers insert malicious SQL code into input fields to manipulate databases. This can lead to unauthorized access to sensitive user data.

ii. Cross-Site Scripting (XSS): This attack involves injecting malicious scripts into web pages viewed by users. When executed, these scripts can steal cookies, session tokens, or sensitive information.

iii. Phishing Attacks: Users are often targeted with deceptive emails or messages that lead them to fake websites, tricking them into providing personal information.

iv. **Malware Distribution:** Malicious software can be embedded within websites, downloading harmful code onto users' devices when they visit.

- User Responsibility in Data Security: While website owners and developers are responsible for securing their platforms, users must also adopt best practices to safeguard their data. Here are key strategies for users:

i. **Strong, Unique Passwords:** Users should create complex passwords that are difficult to guess and use different passwords for different accounts. Password managers can help securely store and generate unique passwords.

ii. **Enable Multi-Factor Authentication (MFA):** MFA adds an extra layer of security by requiring a second form of verification, such as a text message or authenticator app. This makes unauthorized access much more difficult, even if passwords are compromised.

iii. **Be Cautious with Links and Downloads:** Users should avoid clicking on suspicious links or downloading files from untrusted sources. Hovering over links to reveal the actual URL can help identify phishing attempts.

iv. **Regularly Update Software:** Keeping operating systems, browsers, and applications up to date ensures that users benefit from the latest security patches, reducing the risk of exploitation through known vulnerabilities.

v. **Understand Privacy Settings:** Users should familiarize themselves with the privacy settings of the websites and applications they use. Limiting the amount of personal data shared can reduce the impact of potential data breaches.

vi. **Monitor Accounts and Credit Reports:** Regularly reviewing bank and credit card statements, as well as credit reports, can help users quickly identify and address unauthorized transactions or activities.

- The Role of Education: User education is essential in the fight against data attacks. Organizations can facilitate this by providing resources and training on cybersecurity awareness. Users should be informed about the types of threats they might face and how to recognize them.

4.4. EMAIL ATTACKS

4.4.1. Fake Email

Fake emails, often referred to as phishing emails, are deceptive messages crafted to trick recipients into providing sensitive information, such as passwords, credit card details, or personal identification. These emails typically impersonate legitimate organizations, making them appear trustworthy. Here's a closer look at how fake emails operate and how to recognize and protect against them.

- Characteristics of Fake Emails:
  i. **Deceptive Sender Addresses:** Phishing emails often come from addresses that look similar to legitimate ones but contain slight variations (e.g., "support@bank-secure.com" instead of "support@bank.com").
  ii. **Urgent Language:** These emails frequently employ a sense of urgency, prompting recipients to act quickly. Phrases like "Your account will be suspended" or "Immediate action required" are common tactics to provoke hasty responses.
  iii. **Poor Grammar and Spelling:** Many fake emails contain grammatical errors or awkward phrasing. Legitimate organizations typically proofread their communications, so these red flags should raise suspicion.
  iv. **Suspicious Links or Attachments:** Phishing emails often include links that lead to fake websites designed to capture login credentials or malicious attachments that can install malware.
- Protecting Against Fake Emails:
  i. **Verify Sender Information:** Always check the sender's email address closely. If something seems off, avoid interacting with the email.
  ii. **Do Not Click Links:** Hover over links to see the actual URL before clicking. If in doubt, navigate directly to the official website by typing the URL into your browser.
  iii. **Look for Personalization:** Legitimate companies usually address you by name. Generic greetings like "Dear Customer" can be a sign of a phishing attempt.
  iv. **Report Suspicious Emails:** If you receive a suspected phishing email, report it to your email provider and the organization being impersonated.

By staying vigilant and informed, users can significantly reduce their risk of falling victim to fake emails and safeguard their sensitive information.

4.4.2. Fake Email Messages as Spam

Fake email messages, often categorized as spam, are a significant issue in today's digital landscape. These deceptive communications can range from harmless advertisements to malicious attempts to deceive recipients into divulging sensitive information. Understanding the characteristics and dangers of fake emails is crucial for users to protect themselves and their information.

- Characteristics of Fake Email Messages:
  - i. **Deceptive Sender Information:** Spam emails frequently use sender addresses that appear legitimate but often contain subtle discrepancies. For instance, an email might come from "support@legitcompany.com" while the actual address is "support@legitcompanie.com." Users should be vigilant about these variations.
  - ii. **Generic Greetings:** Fake emails typically use impersonal salutations like "Dear Customer" instead of addressing recipients by name. Legitimate companies often personalize their communications.
  - iii. **Urgent Language and Threats:** Many fake emails create a false sense of urgency. Phrases like "Immediate action required" or "Your account has been compromised" are designed to provoke panic and prompt hasty decisions.
  - iv. **Suspicious Links and Attachments:** Phishing attempts often include links that lead to fraudulent websites or attachments containing malware. Users should be cautious about clicking on these links, especially if the email seems suspicious.
  - v. **Poor Language Quality:** Fake emails often contain grammatical errors, awkward phrasing, and spelling mistakes. While legitimate companies usually have professional communications, spam messages often lack attention to detail.
- Types of Spam Emails:
  - i. **Phishing Emails:** These messages attempt to trick recipients into providing personal information, such as usernames, passwords, or financial details. They often impersonate banks, online services, or well-known companies.

ii. **Nigerian Prince Scams:** A classic form of scam where recipients are promised large sums of money in exchange for assistance in transferring funds. These emails play on greed and often include elaborate backstories.

iii. **Lottery and Prize Scams:** Users receive emails claiming they've won a lottery or prize, but they must pay a fee or provide personal information to claim it. These are often fraudulent.

iv. **Tech Support Scams:** These messages claim to be from tech companies alerting users to viruses or malware on their computers. They typically offer assistance but are aimed at extracting payment or personal data.

- Protecting Against Fake Email Messages:

i. **Use Spam Filters:** Most email providers offer built-in spam filters that automatically detect and filter out suspicious messages. Regularly check your spam folder to ensure important emails haven't been incorrectly marked.

ii. **Verify Sender Information:** Always scrutinize the sender's email address before responding or clicking on links. If the email is unexpected, it's wise to contact the organization directly using official contact details.

iii. **Avoid Clicking Links:** Instead of clicking links in emails, manually type the website URL into your browser. This reduces the risk of being directed to a fraudulent site.

iv. **Educate Yourself:** Familiarize yourself with common phishing tactics and stay informed about the latest scams. Awareness is your first line of defense.

v. **Report Spam:** If you receive a spam email, report it to your email provider. This helps improve spam filters and protects other users.

4.4.3. Fake (Inaccurate) Email Header Data

Email headers contain crucial information about the origin, routing, and content of an email message. They help email clients determine where the message came from and how to display it. However, cybercriminals often manipulate email header data to deceive recipients, making it essential for users to understand how to identify and interpret this information.

- What is an Email Header?: An email header is a portion of an email that includes details about the sender, recipient, subject, and the path the email took through the internet. It typically consists of various fields, such as:
  - i. **From:** The email address of the sender.
  - ii. **To:** The recipient's email address.
  - iii. **Subject:** The topic of the email.
  - iv. **Date:** When the email was sent.
  - v. **Received:** Information about the servers that handled the email.
- How Headers can be Manipulated?: Cybercriminals can easily forge email headers, making it appear as if the email comes from a trusted source. Here are common techniques they use:
  - i. **Spoofing:** This involves changing the "From" address to make it look like the email is from a legitimate source. For example, an email may appear to come from a well-known company, but the actual sender's address may be completely different.
  - ii. **Using Legitimate Services:** Attackers can use compromised accounts or legitimate email services to send phishing emails. This makes it harder for recipients to identify the email as malicious.
  - iii. **Altering the Subject and Content:** Even if the header appears legitimate, the content can include links or attachments that lead to phishing sites or malware downloads.
- Risks Associated with Inaccurate Email Headers:
  - i. **Phishing Attacks:** Fake headers are commonly used in phishing attempts, where attackers try to trick users into revealing personal information. Users may unwittingly provide their credentials, believing they are interacting with a trusted entity.
  - ii. **Malware Distribution:** Emails with manipulated headers can contain malicious attachments or links. When users click these, they may inadvertently download malware onto their devices.
  - iii. **Identity Theft:** If attackers successfully impersonate a trusted source, they can gather sensitive personal information, leading to identity theft.

- Identifying Fake Email Headers: To protect against fake emails, users should learn to analyze email headers. Here are key steps:
  i. **Check the "From" Address:** Scrutinize the sender's email address. Look for minor misspellings or unusual domains that may indicate a scam.
  ii. **Review the "Received" Lines:** The "Received" section of the header shows the path the email took. By checking these lines, users can identify inconsistencies in the email's routing that may suggest spoofing.
  iii. **Look for DKIM and SPF Records:** DomainKeys Identified Mail (DKIM) and Sender Policy Framework (SPF) are authentication methods used to verify that an email is coming from a legitimate source. If these records are missing or fail, it could indicate a problem.
  iv. **Use Online Tools:** Various online tools can help analyze email headers and identify potential issues. These tools can simplify the process of understanding the information in the headers.

4.4.4. Phishing

Phishing is a cybercrime that involves tricking individuals into providing sensitive information, such as usernames, passwords, credit card numbers, and personal identification details. Cybercriminals use deceptive emails, messages, or websites that appear legitimate to lure victims into revealing their information. This fraudulent practice can lead to identity theft, financial loss, and significant security breaches.

- **How Phishing Works?:** Phishing attacks typically follow a common pattern:
  i. **Crafting Deceptive Messages:** Attackers create emails or messages that mimic legitimate organizations, such as banks, social media platforms, or e-commerce sites. They often use official logos, language, and formatting to create a sense of authenticity.
  ii. **Creating a Sense of Urgency:** Many phishing messages employ tactics that create urgency, encouraging recipients to act quickly. Phrases like "Your account will be suspended unless you verify your information immediately" or "You've won a prize, but you must claim it now" are common.

iii. **Providing a Malicious Link:** The message typically contains a link that directs the user to a fake website designed to resemble a legitimate one. When users enter their information on this fraudulent site, attackers capture it for malicious use.

iv. **Exploiting Trust:** Attackers often exploit users' trust in recognizable brands or institutions, making them more likely to comply with requests for sensitive information.

- Types of Phishing Attacks:

i. **Email Phishing:** The most common form, where attackers send fraudulent emails to a large number of recipients.

ii. **Spear Phishing:** This targeted approach focuses on specific individuals or organizations. Attackers gather personal information to craft tailored messages that increase the likelihood of success.

iii. **Whaling:** A type of spear phishing aimed at high-profile targets, such as executives or key decision-makers within a company. These attacks often involve more sophisticated tactics.

iv. **SMS Phishing (Smishing):** Involves sending fraudulent text messages that contain links to malicious sites or prompts for sensitive information.

v. **Voice Phishing (Vishing):** Attackers use phone calls to impersonate legitimate entities, convincing victims to provide personal information.

- Consequences of Phishing: The impact of a successful phishing attack can be severe:

i. **Identity Theft:** Personal information acquired through phishing can be used to impersonate victims, leading to unauthorized access to accounts or financial fraud.

ii. **Financial Loss:** Victims may suffer direct financial loss through stolen funds or indirect losses from identity restoration efforts.

iii. **Reputational Damage:** Organizations falling victim to phishing attacks can face reputational harm, loss of customer trust, and potential legal repercussions.

iv. **Data Breaches:** Phishing can serve as an entry point for more significant cyberattacks, potentially leading to extensive data breaches.

- Protecting Against Phishing: To mitigate the risks associated with phishing, individuals and organizations can take several proactive steps:
  i. **Educate Users:** Regular training on recognizing phishing attempts can significantly reduce the likelihood of falling victim to these scams.
  ii. **Verify Sender Information:** Always scrutinize email addresses and messages. Look for signs of deception, such as unusual sender addresses or generic greetings.
  iii. **Avoid Clicking Links:** Instead of clicking on links in emails or messages, type the URL directly into the browser. This helps ensure users are accessing the legitimate site.
  iv. **Use Multi-Factor Authentication (MFA):** Implementing MFA adds an extra layer of security, making it more difficult for attackers to access accounts even if they acquire login credentials.
  v. **Report Suspicious Activity:** Encourage users to report phishing attempts to their IT department or email providers. This can help prevent others from falling victim to similar attacks.

4.4.5. Protecting Against Email Attacks

Email is a primary communication tool in both personal and professional contexts, making it a prime target for cyberattacks. Phishing, malware, and other forms of email attacks can lead to severe consequences, including data breaches and financial loss. Here's a comprehensive guide on how to protect against email attacks effectively.

- Understanding Email Attacks:
  i. **Phishing:** Attackers impersonate legitimate organizations to trick users into revealing sensitive information or downloading malware.
  ii. **Spear Phishing:** This targeted approach involves customizing messages for specific individuals or organizations, often using information gathered from social media.
  iii. **Malware:** Malicious attachments or links in emails can install harmful software on a user's device, leading to data theft or system compromise.

iv. **Business Email Compromise (BEC):** Attackers pose as executives or trusted partners to manipulate employees into transferring funds or sensitive information.

- Best Practices for Protection:

i. Implement Strong Security Measures:

a. **Use Strong Passwords:** Create complex passwords that include a mix of letters, numbers, and special characters. Avoid using easily guessable information such as birthdays or common words.

b. **Enable Multi-Factor Authentication (MFA):** MFA adds an additional layer of security by requiring users to verify their identity through a second method, such as a text message or authenticator app.

ii. Educate and Train Users:

a. **Regular Training:** Conduct training sessions on recognizing email threats. Users should learn to identify phishing attempts, suspicious attachments, and other red flags.

b. **Simulated Phishing Tests:** Run simulated phishing campaigns to assess and improve user awareness. Provide feedback and additional training based on results.

iii. Utilize Advanced Email Security Solutions:

a. **Spam Filters:** Implement robust spam filtering to detect and block phishing attempts and malicious emails before they reach users' inboxes.

b. **Email Authentication Protocols:** Utilize technologies like SPF (Sender Policy Framework), DKIM (DomainKeys Identified Mail), and DMARC (Domain-based Message Authentication, Reporting and Conformance) to validate email senders and prevent spoofing.

iv. Be Cautious with Links and Attachments:

a. **Hover Over Links:** Before clicking on links in emails, hover over them to preview the actual URL. If it looks suspicious or unfamiliar, do not click.

b. **Scan Attachments:** Use antivirus software to scan email attachments before opening them, especially if they come from unknown sources.

v. Regularly Update Software:

a **Keep Software Up to Date:** Ensure that all operating systems, email clients, and antivirus programs are updated regularly. Software updates often include security patches that protect against vulnerabilities.

vi. Establish Clear Communication Protocols:

a. **Verify Requests for Sensitive Information:** Encourage users to verify any requests for sensitive information or financial transactions through direct communication methods, such as a phone call.

b. **Use Secure Communication Channels:** For sensitive discussions, consider using encrypted messaging services instead of email.

vii. Monitor and Respond to Threats:

a. **Continuous Monitoring:** Implement tools that monitor email accounts for unusual activity, such as logins from unfamiliar locations or changes to account settings.

b. **Incident Response Plan:** Develop a response plan for email attacks. This should include steps for reporting suspicious emails, containing potential breaches, and notifying affected parties.

CHAPTER 5

OPERATING SYSTEMS

Contents

5.1. SECURITY IN OPERATING SYSTEMS

Security in operating systems (OS) is critical for protecting data, applications, and overall system integrity. Operating systems serve as the foundation for software applications and user interactions, making their security paramount. Here are key aspects of OS security:

1. User Authentication and Access Control: Strong user authentication mechanisms are essential for ensuring that only authorized users can access the system. Multi-factor

authentication (MFA) enhances security by requiring users to provide multiple forms of verification. Additionally, access control measures, such as role-based access control (RBAC), help limit user permissions, ensuring users only have access to necessary resources.

2. System Updates and Patch Management: Regular updates and patch management are vital for protecting against vulnerabilities. Operating system vendors frequently release patches to address security flaws. Organizations must implement a robust update strategy to ensure systems are consistently protected against known threats.
3. File System Permissions: Operating systems utilize file system permissions to restrict access to sensitive files and directories. By setting appropriate permissions, administrators can control who can read, write, or execute files, thereby protecting critical data from unauthorized access or modification.
4. Malware Protection: Operating systems should incorporate tools for detecting and mitigating malware. This includes built-in antivirus features, real-time scanning, and mechanisms to prevent the execution of untrusted applications.
5. Intrusion Detection and Logging: Implementing intrusion detection systems (IDS) and maintaining comprehensive logs are essential for monitoring system activities and detecting potential security breaches. Logs provide valuable insights for forensic analysis and can help identify suspicious behavior.
6. Secure Boot and Virtualization: Secure boot mechanisms ensure that only trusted software can run during the system startup process. Additionally, virtualization technologies can create isolated environments for applications, reducing the risk of system-wide compromises.

5.1.1. A Bit of History

The history of security in operating systems (OS) reflects the evolution of computing technology and the increasing sophistication of threats. Here's a brief overview of key milestones in OS security:

1. Early Days (1960s–1970s): In the early days of computing, systems were primarily used in academic and government institutions. Security was often minimal, as computers were large, expensive, and used by trusted personnel. Basic access controls were introduced, but

vulnerabilities were largely overlooked due to the limited number of users.

2. Multics Project (1965): The Multics (multiplexed information and computing service) project was one of the first attempts to create a secure operating system. It introduced concepts such as hierarchical file systems, user authentication, and access controls. While never fully adopted, Multics influenced future OS designs, including UNIX.
3. UNIX and Security Models (1970s): UNIX, developed in the early 1970s, implemented several security features, including user accounts and file permissions. The concept of user groups and the discretionary access control model (DAC) emerged, allowing users to set permissions on their files.
4. Rise of Malware (1980s): As personal computers became more common, malware began to emerge. The first known computer virus, "Creeper," appeared in the early 1970s, but the 1980s saw a surge in viruses and worms, prompting the need for enhanced security measures.
5. Windows and NT Security (1990s): Microsoft introduced Windows NT, which incorporated significant security features, such as Kerberos authentication and a more robust permissions model. This era marked the beginning of security becoming a focal point in OS development, as enterprises increasingly relied on Windows systems.
6. Security Standards (2000s): The establishment of security standards, such as Common Criteria and the ISO/IEC 27001, provided frameworks for evaluating and improving OS security. The introduction of features like firewalls, antivirus software, and automatic updates became common practices.
7. Modern Challenges (2010s–Present): The rise of cloud computing and mobile devices has introduced new security challenges. Operating systems for these platforms, such as Android and iOS, have developed sandboxing techniques to isolate applications and enhance security. Moreover, incidents like the Stuxnet worm and various data breaches have highlighted the necessity for ongoing improvements in OS security.

5.1.2. Protected Objects

Protected objects in operating systems are essential for enforcing security and ensuring that resources are accessed and manipulated in a controlled manner.

The concept revolves around the idea of restricting access to certain objects, such as files, memory, and devices, to authorized users or processes. Here's an overview of how protected objects function and their significance in OS security:

1. Definition of Protected Objects: Protected objects are any resources managed by the operating system that require protection from unauthorized access or modification. This includes:
    i. **Files and Directories:** Protection mechanisms ensure that only authorized users can read, write, or execute files.
    ii. **Memory Segments:** Memory protection prevents processes from accessing each other's memory spaces, which is crucial for stability and security.
    iii. **Devices:** Hardware devices, such as printers and network interfaces, are protected to ensure only authorized processes can interact with them.
2. Access Control Mechanisms: Access control is fundamental to protecting objects. Common mechanisms include:
    i. **Discretionary Access Control (DAC):** Users have the ability to set permissions for their objects, determining who can access or modify them. This is seen in file systems where file owners can grant or revoke access.
    ii. **Mandatory Access Control (MAC):** The system enforces access controls based on predefined policies, irrespective of user settings. This is often used in environments requiring higher security, such as military systems.
    iii. **Role-Based Access Control (RBAC):** Permissions are assigned based on user roles within an organization, streamlining access management while maintaining security.
3. Security Models: Several security models have been developed to guide the implementation of protection mechanisms:
    i. **Bell-LaPadula Model:** Focuses on maintaining data confidentiality. It prevents users from accessing data at a higher security level (no read up) and prevents unauthorized disclosure (no write down).
    ii. **Biba Model:** Aims to maintain data integrity, ensuring that subjects cannot write to a lower integrity level (no write down) and can only read from higher levels (no read up).

iii. **Clark-Wilson Model:** Emphasizes well-formed transactions and separation of duties, ensuring that data integrity is maintained through controlled access and verified transactions.

4. Implementation Techniques:

i. **Access Control Lists (ACLs)**: These specify which users or groups have permissions to access specific objects, detailing the types of operations they can perform (read, write, execute).

ii. **Capabilities:** Instead of using ACLs, some systems implement capabilities, which are tokens that grant specific permissions to users or processes for certain objects.

5. Memory Protection: These techniques ensure that processes cannot read or write to memory segments they do not own. This is achieved through:

i. **Segmentation:** Dividing memory into segments, each with its own access rights.

ii. **Paging:** Dividing memory into fixed-size pages, controlling access to each page and preventing processes from accessing pages allocated to others.

6. Importance in OS Security: Protected objects are vital for:

i. **Preventing Unauthorized Access:** Ensures that sensitive data remains confidential and is accessed only by authorized users.

ii. **Maintaining System Stability:** Prevents rogue processes from interfering with each other or accessing critical system resources.

iii. **Supporting Compliance:** Helps organizations meet regulatory requirements regarding data protection and privacy.

5.1.3. Operating System Tools to Implement Security Functions

Operating systems (OS) offer a variety of tools and features to implement security functions, helping to protect data, maintain system integrity, and manage user access. Here are some key tools and features available in modern operating systems:

1. User Authentication: Most operating systems provide authentication mechanisms, such as password-based logins, biometric verification (fingerprints, facial recognition), and multi-factor authentication (MFA). These tools ensure that only authorized users can access the system.

2. Access Control Lists (ACLs): ACLs are used to define permissions for files, directories, and resources. By specifying which users or groups have what level of access (read, write, execute), ACLs help manage who can interact with specific objects within the system.
3. Firewalls: Many operating systems come with built-in firewalls that monitor and control incoming and outgoing network traffic. These firewalls can block unauthorized access and protect against various network-based attacks.
4. Encryption Tools: Operating systems often include encryption features for securing data at rest and in transit. Tools like BitLocker (Windows) and FileVault (macOS) encrypt entire drives, while others allow users to encrypt individual files or folders.
5. Intrusion Detection Systems (IDS): Some OS provide integrated intrusion detection capabilities that monitor system activities for suspicious behavior. These tools can alert administrators to potential security breaches or policy violations.
6. System Logging and Auditing: Operating systems maintain logs of system events, user activities, and access attempts. These logs are crucial for monitoring system health, troubleshooting issues, and conducting forensic investigations after security incidents.
7. Update Management Tools: Regularly updating software and the OS itself is critical for security. Most operating systems offer automatic update features that help ensure users receive the latest security patches.

5.2. SECURITY IN THE DESIGN OF OPERATING SYSTEMS

Security in the design of operating systems (OS) is crucial for protecting data and ensuring system integrity. An effective OS must integrate security principles from the ground up, rather than as an afterthought. Here are key considerations in designing secure operating systems:

1. Principle of Least Privilege: This principle mandates that users and processes should have the minimum level of access necessary to perform their tasks. By limiting permissions, the potential impact of malicious activities or accidental misuse is reduced.
2. Secure Boot Processes: Designing secure boot mechanisms ensures that only trusted and verified software is loaded during system

startup. This prevents unauthorized code from executing, protecting the system from rootkits and other malware.

3. Access Control Models: Implementing robust access control models, such as Discretionary Access Control (DAC), Mandatory Access Control (MAC), or Role-Based Access Control (RBAC), helps manage user permissions and protect sensitive resources. These models define who can access what data and under what conditions.
4. Data Protection Mechanisms: Incorporating encryption for data at rest and in transit safeguards sensitive information from unauthorized access. Strong cryptographic practices should be embedded in the OS design to ensure data confidentiality and integrity.
5. Secure APIs and Libraries: Designing secure application programming interfaces (APIs) and libraries minimizes vulnerabilities. Developers should follow secure coding practices to prevent common exploits like buffer overflows and injection attacks.
6. Regular Security Audits: OS designs should facilitate regular security audits and assessments. This includes incorporating logging and monitoring features that track system activities, enabling the detection of suspicious behavior.
7. Patch Management: The OS should include mechanisms for easy and automated patch management, ensuring that vulnerabilities are addressed promptly through updates.

5.2.1. Simplicity of Design

Simplicity of design is a fundamental principle in creating secure and efficient operating systems. A simpler design reduces complexity, making it easier to understand, implement, and maintain security features. Here are key benefits of simplicity in OS design:

1. Reduced Attack Surface: Fewer components and simpler interactions mean there are fewer potential vulnerabilities for attackers to exploit. By minimizing unnecessary features, the risk of security flaws is significantly lowered.
2. Ease of Understanding: A straightforward design allows developers and administrators to better grasp the system's architecture and functionality. This understanding is crucial for identifying security weaknesses and implementing appropriate measures.
3. Faster Debugging and Maintenance: Simplicity streamlines troubleshooting processes. When issues arise, simpler systems can

be analyzed and resolved more quickly, reducing downtime and potential security exposure.

4. Enhanced User Experience: A simpler interface often leads to better usability, allowing users to navigate the system without confusion. This reduces the likelihood of user errors, which can lead to security breaches.
5. Streamlined Security Policies: Clear and concise design aids in establishing effective security policies. When systems are easy to manage, enforcing and auditing security measures becomes more efficient.

5.2.2. Layered Design

Layered design is a crucial architectural principle in operating systems that enhances security, modularity, and maintainability. By organizing components into distinct layers, each with specific responsibilities, this approach provides several benefits:

1. Separation of Concerns: Each layer focuses on a specific aspect of system functionality, such as hardware management, system calls, and user interfaces. This separation allows developers to work on individual layers without affecting others, making it easier to manage and update the system.
2. Enhanced Security: Layered design restricts interactions between layers, allowing for controlled access to sensitive resources. Security measures can be implemented at various layers, helping to mitigate vulnerabilities and protect critical data.
3. Modularity and Reusability: Layers can be developed and tested independently, promoting modularity. This modularity enables the reuse of components across different systems or versions, streamlining development processes.
4. Simplified Debugging and Maintenance: When issues arise, the layered architecture allows for targeted troubleshooting within specific layers. This simplification makes identifying and resolving problems more efficient, reducing downtime.
5. Scalability: Layered systems can be more easily scaled, as new layers or components can be added to enhance functionality without overhauling the entire architecture.

5.2.3. Kernelized Design

Kernelized design refers to an architectural approach in operating systems where core functionalities are centralized within a minimal kernel. This design emphasizes efficiency, security, and performance. Here are its key features and benefits:

1. Minimalism: A kernelized design keeps the kernel small by only including essential functions, such as process management, memory management, and hardware abstraction. This reduces complexity and the potential for vulnerabilities.
2. Performance: By centralizing critical functions in the kernel, communication between hardware and software can occur more quickly, improving overall system performance. This is especially beneficial for time-sensitive applications.
3. Security: A minimal kernel reduces the attack surface, making it harder for malicious entities to exploit vulnerabilities. Security features can be tightly integrated into the kernel, ensuring better control over system resources.
4. Efficient Resource Management: Kernelized designs facilitate direct access to hardware resources, optimizing how processes interact with the system. This leads to better resource allocation and management.
5. Modularity: While the kernel handles core functions, additional services can run in user space. This modularity allows developers to enhance system capabilities without compromising kernel stability.

5.2.4. Reference Monitor

A reference monitor is a crucial component in operating system security, serving as a conceptual framework that enforces access control policies. It mediates all access requests to sensitive resources, ensuring that only authorized actions are permitted. Here are the key aspects of the reference monitor:

1. Centralized Access Control: The reference monitor acts as a gatekeeper for all interactions between subjects (users or processes) and objects (files, devices, or memory). By centralizing access control, it ensures consistent enforcement of security policies throughout the system.
2. Complete Mediation: For effective security, the reference monitor must mediate all access attempts without exception. This means that every request to access a resource must pass through the reference monitor, which evaluates whether the request adheres to predefined security policies.

3. Tamper-Proof: A critical aspect of the reference monitor is that it must be protected from unauthorized modifications. This tamper-proof nature is essential for maintaining trust in the security enforcement mechanism, preventing attackers from bypassing it.
4. Logging and Auditing: The reference monitor can also maintain logs of access attempts, both successful and unsuccessful. This logging capability is vital for auditing purposes, enabling system administrators to analyze security events and detect potential breaches.
5. Policy Implementation: The reference monitor operates based on a set of security policies, which can be defined using various models, such as discretionary access control (DAC) or mandatory access control (MAC). These policies dictate the permissions and restrictions for users and processes interacting with resources.

5.2.5. Correctness and Completeness

Correctness and completeness are critical concepts in the context of security models and access control mechanisms within operating systems:

1. Correctness: It refers to the accuracy and reliability of a security model in enforcing specific policies. A security system is considered correct if it enforces all defined access control rules consistently and accurately. This means that all legitimate access requests are granted, and all unauthorized requests are denied. For instance, if a user with specific permissions can access a resource, the system must allow that access; conversely, if a user lacks the necessary permissions, access must be correctly denied. Ensuring correctness involves rigorous testing and validation of the security mechanisms to confirm that they function as intended.
2. Completeness: On the other hand, refers to the system's ability to enforce all specified policies without exception. A complete security model ensures that every possible access attempt is evaluated against the defined policies. This means there are no gaps or loopholes that could be exploited to bypass security measures. For example, if a policy states that only certain users can access sensitive data, completeness ensures that all access requests are checked against this policy, including edge cases and potential vulnerabilities.

5.2.6. Secure Design Principles

Secure design principles are essential guidelines that help developers create systems resilient to threats and vulnerabilities. Adhering to these principles throughout the software development lifecycle can significantly enhance the security posture of an application or system. Here are some key secure design principles:

1. Least Privilege: The principle of least privilege dictates that users and processes should only have the minimum access necessary to perform their tasks. This limits potential damage from compromised accounts or applications, as attackers gain access to fewer resources.
2. Fail-Safe Defaults: Systems should be designed to deny access by default, allowing only explicit permissions. This fail-safe approach ensures that unauthorized access is minimized, requiring intentional actions to grant access to resources.
3. Separation of Duties: Dividing responsibilities among different individuals or processes reduces the risk of fraud or malicious activity. By ensuring that no single user has control over all aspects of a sensitive operation, the potential for abuse is minimized.
4. Defense in Depth: Implementing multiple layers of security controls provides redundancy. If one layer fails, additional layers still protect the system. This can include firewalls, intrusion detection systems, and data encryption, creating a more resilient security posture.
5. Input Validation: All inputs must be validated and sanitized to prevent common vulnerabilities, such as SQL injection and cross-site scripting (XSS). This principle helps ensure that only legitimate data is processed by the system.
6. Security through Obscurity: While not a standalone security measure, obscuring system details (like implementation specifics) can provide an additional layer of protection. However, it should not be relied upon as the primary means of securing a system.
7. Audit and Logging: Incorporating auditing and logging features allows for monitoring of system activities. This capability helps detect suspicious behavior, facilitates forensic analysis after incidents, and supports compliance with regulatory requirements.
8. Regular Updates and Patching: Keeping software and systems updated with the latest security patches is critical for mitigating known vulnerabilities. A proactive approach to updates reduces the risk of exploitation.

5.2.7. Trusted Systems

Trusted systems are designed to ensure a high level of security and integrity, capable of protecting sensitive information from unauthorized access and manipulation. These systems adhere to stringent security principles and frameworks, often implemented in environments where data confidentiality, integrity, and availability are paramount.

1. Definition and Purpose: A trusted system is defined as one that can be trusted to enforce its security policies consistently and reliably. This trust is established through rigorous design, implementation, and verification processes that demonstrate the system's ability to protect against threats.
2. Key Characteristics:
   - **i. Security Policy Enforcement:** Trusted systems implement clear and robust security policies, ensuring that access controls are strictly enforced. These policies dictate who can access what resources and under what conditions.
   - **ii. Complete Mediation:** Every access request is checked against the security policy, ensuring that no actions can bypass security measures.
   - **iii. Minimal Trusted Computing Base (TCB):** The TCB consists of the components that are critical to enforcing the security policy. A smaller TCB reduces the potential attack surface, making it easier to validate and secure.
3. Evaluation Standards: Trusted systems are often evaluated against established criteria, such as the Common Criteria for Information Technology Security Evaluation (CC) or the Trusted Computer System Evaluation Criteria (TCSEC, also known as the Orange Book). These frameworks provide guidelines for assessing the security of a system.
4. Examples of Trusted Systems: Common examples include systems used in military applications, financial institutions, and healthcare environments, where the protection of sensitive data is critical.

5.2.8. Trusted System Functions

Trusted systems are designed with specific functions that enhance their security and reliability, making them capable of protecting sensitive information and ensuring compliance with established security policies. Here are some of the key functions of trusted systems:

1. Access Control: Trusted systems implement robust access control mechanisms to manage who can access what resources. This includes user authentication and authorization processes, ensuring that only authorized users can perform specific actions. Access controls can be based on roles, attributes, or predefined policies.
2. Audit and Monitoring: Effective audit functions are crucial for tracking system activities. Trusted systems maintain detailed logs of access attempts, modifications, and other significant events. This auditing capability helps detect suspicious behavior, facilitates forensic investigations, and ensures compliance with regulatory requirements.
3. Data Integrity and Confidentiality: Trusted systems employ encryption and integrity checks to protect sensitive data both at rest and in transit. By ensuring that data is not altered or accessed by unauthorized entities, these systems maintain confidentiality and integrity.
4. Complete Mediation: Every access request must be evaluated against the security policies of the system. Trusted systems ensure complete mediation, meaning that all requests for access to resources are checked, preventing unauthorized actions from bypassing security measures.
5. System Recovery: In the event of a security breach or system failure, trusted systems include recovery functions that allow for the restoration of operations. This may involve backup procedures, system snapshots, and secure restoration processes to ensure business continuity.
6. Configuration Management: Trusted systems maintain strict configuration management practices, ensuring that any changes to the system are logged and controlled. This function helps prevent unauthorized modifications that could compromise security.

5.2.9. The Results of Trusted Systems Research

Trusted systems research focuses on enhancing security, reliability, and integrity in computing environments. Key results include the development of frameworks and models that establish trust in hardware and software components. Techniques such as Trusted Platform Modules (TPMs) and secure boot processes have been pivotal in creating a trustworthy computing foundation. Research has also led to the advancement of access control mechanisms and cryptographic protocols, ensuring data confidentiality and user privacy. Additionally, the use of formal methods in verifying system properties has increased the assurance that systems function as intended without vulnerabilities. Collaborative efforts between academia and industry have resulted in real-world applications, such as secure cloud computing and Internet of Things (IoT) security measures. Furthermore, methodologies for risk assessment and threat modeling have been refined, allowing organizations to better understand and mitigate potential security risks.

Overall, trusted systems research continues to evolve, addressing emerging challenges in cybersecurity while promoting a secure digital ecosystem. Its impact is evident in the increasing reliance on trusted technologies across various sectors, enhancing user confidence and safeguarding critical information.

5.3. ROOTKIT

A rootkit is a type of malicious software designed to gain unauthorized access to a computer or network while hiding its presence from users and security programs. The term "rootkit" derives from "root," the highest level of access in Unix-based systems, and "kit," which refers to the software components that enable the exploitation of system vulnerabilities.

Rootkits can be used for various malicious purposes, including stealing sensitive information, manipulating system operations, or creating backdoors for future access. They often operate at a low level in the operating system, allowing them to bypass standard security measures. There are several types of rootkits, including:

1. **User-Mode Rootkits:** These run in the user space and can be easier to detect than kernel-mode rootkits. They typically modify applications and processes to gain unauthorized access.
2. **Kernel-Mode Rootkits:** These operate at the kernel level, making them harder to detect because they can intercept system calls and manipulate system behavior directly.
3. **Bootkits:** A subtype of kernel-mode rootkits that infect the bootloader or operating system kernel, ensuring they are loaded before the operating system starts. This allows them to maintain control over the system.
4. **Firmware Rootkits:** These target firmware, which is the software that runs on hardware devices. They can persist even after the operating system is reinstalled.

Detection of rootkits can be challenging due to their stealthy nature. Traditional antivirus software may struggle to identify them, as rootkits often disguise their files and processes. Tools specifically designed for rootkit detection, like rootkit scanners, can help identify suspicious activities and anomalies.

The removal of rootkits typically requires specialized tools or, in severe cases, a complete reinstallation of the operating system. Preventative measures include maintaining up-to-date software, using strong passwords, and employing security tools that specifically target rootkits. By understanding rootkits and their operations, users can better protect their systems from these covert threats.

5.3.1. Phone Rootkit

A phone rootkit is a type of malicious software specifically designed to infiltrate mobile devices, gaining unauthorized access and control while evading detection. Similar to traditional rootkits for computers, phone rootkits exploit vulnerabilities in the operating system, allowing attackers to manipulate or steal data, monitor user activity, or install additional malware.

Phone rootkits can target both Android and iOS devices, though they often utilize different methods due to the distinct architectures of these operating systems. For Android devices, attackers might exploit security loopholes or use social engineering techniques, such as deceptive apps, to install the rootkit. Once installed, the rootkit can hide its presence by masking processes, files, and even network traffic, making it difficult for users and standard security applications to detect.

For iOS devices, while rootkits are rarer due to the platform's stricter security measures, jailbroken devices are particularly vulnerable. Attackers may leverage jailbreak exploits to gain root access, installing rootkits that can track calls, messages, and location.

Detecting phone rootkits can be challenging, as they often operate stealthily and mimic legitimate system processes. Users can protect themselves by keeping their operating systems updated, avoiding suspicious apps, and utilizing mobile security solutions that specifically include rootkit detection features. Regularly monitoring device behavior for unusual activity can also help in identifying potential infections early. Overall, awareness and proactive security measures are essential in safeguarding mobile devices against these covert threats.

5.3.2. Rootkit Evades Detection

Rootkits are designed to evade detection by employing various stealth techniques, making them particularly insidious forms of malware. Their primary goal is to gain unauthorized access to a system while remaining hidden from users and security software. Here are some common methods rootkits use to avoid detection:

1. **Process Hiding:** Rootkits can manipulate the operating system to hide their processes from system monitoring tools. By intercepting system calls, they can ensure that their malicious processes do not appear in task managers or other monitoring applications.
2. **File and Registry Manipulation:** Rootkits often disguise their files or alter system files and registry entries to avoid detection. They may rename malicious files to look like legitimate system files or change their attributes to make them invisible.
3. **Kernel-Level Operations:** Kernel-mode rootkits operate at a low level within the operating system, allowing them to manipulate system behavior directly. This enables them to bypass standard security measures that operate in user mode.
4. **Network Traffic Obfuscation:** Some rootkits can obscure their network activity, disguising command and control communications as legitimate traffic. This makes it harder for network monitoring tools to detect abnormal behavior.
5. **Persistence Mechanisms:** Rootkits often employ techniques to ensure they remain on the system even after reboots, such as altering startup scripts or using bootkits to infect the boot process.

Because of these tactics, detecting and removing rootkits requires specialized tools and techniques. Users are encouraged to maintain updated security software and regularly monitor system behavior for signs of compromise.

5.3.3. Rootkit Operates Unchecked

A rootkit operates unchecked by exploiting system vulnerabilities and gaining unauthorized access while remaining hidden from users and security software. Once installed, a rootkit can control a compromised system with little to no oversight, leading to severe security risks.

Rootkits typically function in two main modes: user-mode and kernel-mode. User-mode rootkits can manipulate user applications, while kernel-mode rootkits gain deeper access to the operating system, allowing them to bypass standard security measures. This level of access enables rootkits to alter system processes, manipulate files, and intercept communications without detection.

The unchecked nature of rootkits allows them to perform various malicious activities, such as stealing sensitive data, logging keystrokes, and installing additional malware. They can also create backdoors for future access, enabling attackers to regain control even after attempts to remove the rootkit.

Detection is challenging due to rootkits' stealth techniques, such as hiding their presence by masking processes and files. Many traditional antivirus solutions struggle to identify them, especially if the rootkit operates at the kernel level.

Because of this unchecked operation, systems infected with rootkits can remain compromised for extended periods, leading to extensive data breaches and loss of privacy. To mitigate these risks, users should employ specialized rootkit detection tools, keep their operating systems and software updated, and adopt proactive security measures. Regular monitoring for unusual system behavior is also crucial in identifying potential rootkit infections before they can cause significant harm.

5.3.4. Sony XCP Rootkit

The Sony XCP rootkit scandal emerged in 2005 when Sony BMG Music Entertainment included a rootkit as part of its digital rights management (DRM) software on certain music CDs. Designed to prevent unauthorized copying, the XCP (Extended Copy Protection) software silently installed itself on users' Windows computers when the CDs were played, without their knowledge or consent.

Once installed, the rootkit operated at a low level in the operating system, making it difficult to detect and remove. It hid files and processes associated with its presence, which raised serious privacy and security concerns. The XCP rootkit inadvertently opened systems to further vulnerabilities, as it could be exploited by other malware due to its deep integration with the operating system.

The scandal escalated when security researchers discovered that the XCP software violated user privacy and created significant security risks. In response to public outcry and lawsuits, Sony stopped using the XCP technology, issued a recall of affected CDs, and released patches to remove the rootkit.

This incident highlighted the dangers of invasive DRM practices and the ethical implications of software that compromises user security. It led to increased scrutiny of software practices in the music industry and emphasized the need for transparency and user consent in software installations. The XCP rootkit remains a cautionary tale about the intersection of digital rights management and user security.

5.3.5. TDSS Rootkits

TDSS rootkits, also known as TDL-4, are a sophisticated family of rootkits that emerged around 2008, primarily targeting Windows operating systems.

Known for their stealth and resilience, TDSS rootkits are often used to facilitate various malicious activities, including data theft, credential harvesting, and the installation of additional malware.

One of the defining features of TDSS rootkits is their ability to operate at the kernel level, allowing them to manipulate core operating system functions. This enables them to hide their presence effectively, making detection by traditional antivirus software difficult. TDSS rootkits can conceal files, processes, and even network traffic, maintaining control over the infected system.

TDSS rootkits often propagate through exploits, such as drive-by downloads, malicious email attachments, or bundled software. Once installed, they create a robust network of infected machines, commonly used in botnets for distributed denial-of-service (DDoS) attacks or spamming campaigns.

Their complexity is further enhanced by the use of encryption and other obfuscation techniques to evade security measures. Additionally, TDSS rootkits may include components that allow remote control, enabling attackers to issue commands and install further payloads.

Detection and removal of TDSS rootkits require specialized tools and techniques, as they often embed themselves deeply into the operating system. Users are encouraged to maintain updated security software, practice safe browsing habits, and perform regular system scans to mitigate the risks posed by these persistent threats. The evolution of TDSS rootkits underscores the ongoing challenges in cybersecurity and the need for advanced detection strategies.

5.3.6. Other Rootkits

Aside from well-known families like TDSS and Sony's XCP, several other rootkits have emerged over the years, each with unique characteristics and methods of operation.

1. **Zeus Rootkit:** Initially designed for stealing banking credentials, the Zeus rootkit operates stealthily to intercept online transactions. It can hide its presence by manipulating system processes and is often distributed through phishing schemes and malicious downloads.
2. **Necurs Rootkit:** Known for its versatility, Necurs can install other malware, including ransomware and keyloggers. It functions as a botnet and is capable of spreading through email attachments and exploit kits, making it a significant threat in the malware landscape.
3. **Stuxnet Rootkit:** While primarily known as a cyberweapon targeting Iran's nuclear facilities, Stuxnet employed rootkit technology to hide its malicious code. It specifically targeted industrial control

systems, demonstrating how rootkits can be used in sophisticated state-sponsored attacks.

4. **Sirefef Rootkit:** This rootkit is often bundled with adware and can hijack web searches, redirecting users to unwanted sites. It is known for its resilience, utilizing complex techniques to avoid detection by antivirus software.

5. **Kernel-Mode Rootkits:** These are generic rootkits that operate at the kernel level, allowing them to control the system's behavior and evade detection. They can be custom-built or derived from open-source code, making them adaptable and potentially harmful.

Overall, rootkits pose significant threats to system integrity and user privacy, necessitating advanced detection methods and proactive security measures to combat them effectively.

CHAPTER 6

NETWORKS

Contents

6.1. NETWORK CONCEPTS

Network concepts encompass the foundational principles and components that enable communication between devices in a network. Understanding these concepts is essential for designing, implementing, and managing network systems effectively (Figures 6.1 and 6.2).

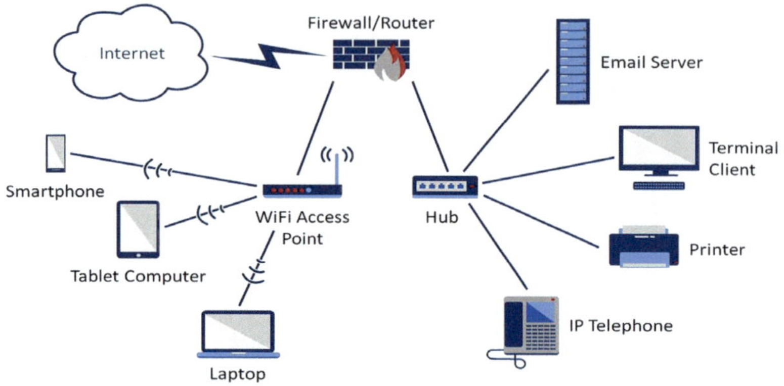

Figure 6.1. Network concepts.

1. **Network Types:** Networks can be categorized into several types, including Local Area Networks (LANs), which connect devices within a limited area (like a home or office), and Wide Area Networks (WANs), which cover larger geographic areas, often connecting multiple LANs. The Internet is the largest example of a WAN.

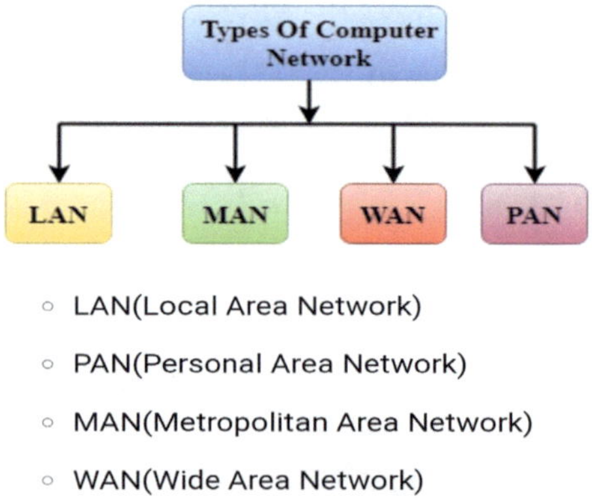

Figure 6.2. Types of computer network.

2. **Protocols:** Communication between devices relies on protocols, which are standardized rules governing data transmission. Common protocols include the Transmission Control Protocol (TCP), which ensures reliable data delivery, and the Internet Protocol (IP), which

handles addressing and routing. The combination of TCP and IP is often referred to as TCP/IP.

3. **IP Addressing:** Each device on a network is assigned a unique IP address, allowing it to be identified and communicated with. IP addresses can be static (permanently assigned) or dynamic (assigned by a DHCP server).
4. **Networking Devices:** Various devices facilitate network connectivity and management, including routers (which direct traffic between networks), switches (which connect devices within a network), and firewalls (which protect networks from unauthorized access) (Figure 6.3).

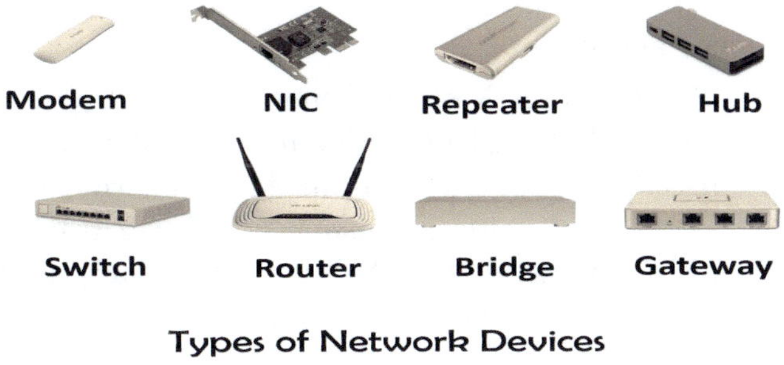

Figure 6.3. Types of networking devices.

5. **Topologies:** Network topology refers to the physical or logical arrangement of devices in a network. Common topologies include star, ring, bus, and mesh, each with its advantages and disadvantages in terms of performance, scalability, and fault tolerance (Figure 6.4).

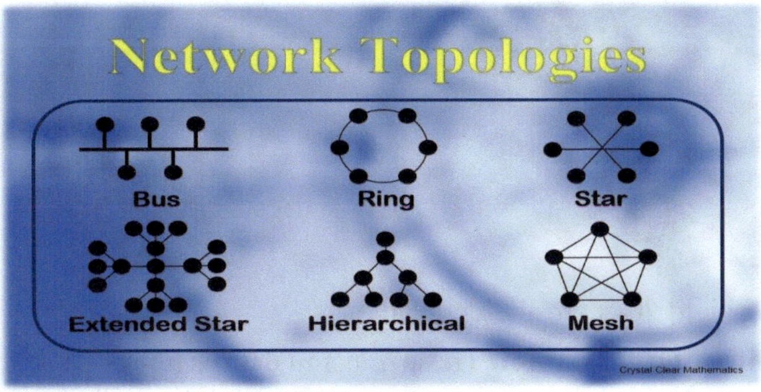

Figure 6.4. Types of network topologies.

6. **Security:** Network security is critical to protecting data and resources from unauthorized access and cyber threats. This includes implementing firewalls, intrusion detection systems, and encryption protocols.

Understanding these core concepts is vital for anyone working in IT or network administration, as they form the basis for building efficient and secure networks.

6.1.1. Background: Network Transmission Media

Network transmission media refers to the physical pathways through which data is transmitted in a network. The choice of transmission media significantly impacts network performance, reliability, and cost. Here are the primary types of network transmission media:

1. Copper Cables:
   i. **Twisted Pair Cable:** Commonly used in LANs, twisted pair cables consist of pairs of insulated copper wires twisted together to reduce electromagnetic interference. They come in two categories: Unshielded Twisted Pair (UTP) and Shielded Twisted Pair (STP). UTP is widely used for Ethernet connections due to its cost-effectiveness.
   ii. **Coaxial Cable:** This type of cable has a central conductor surrounded by insulation, a metallic shield, and an outer layer. Coaxial cables were historically used for cable television and can carry signals over longer distances than twisted pair cables (Figure 6.5).

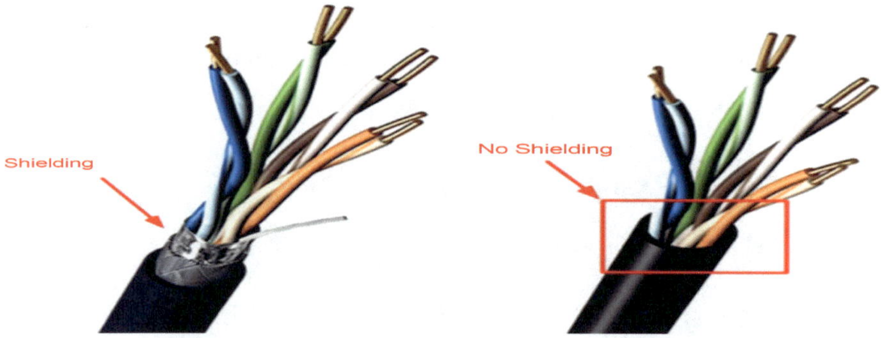

Figure 6.5. Shielded vs. unshielded cable.

2. **Fiber Optic Cables:** These transmit data as light signals through thin strands of glass or plastic. They offer high bandwidth and can cover long distances without signal degradation. Fiber optics are immune to electromagnetic interference, making them ideal for high-speed

and secure data transmission. They are commonly used in backbone networks and long-haul telecommunications (Figure 6.6).

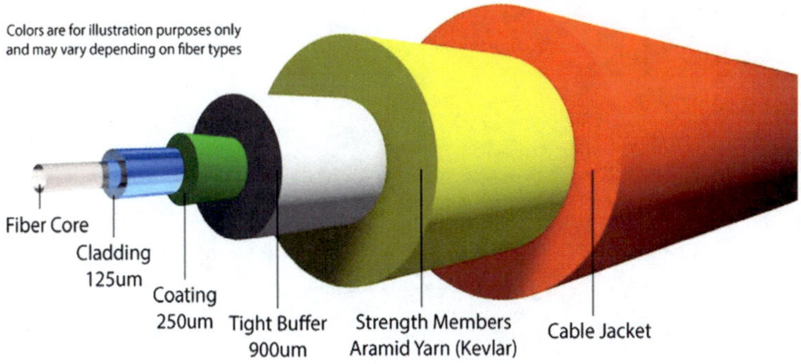

Figure 6.6. *Fiber optic cable.*

3. **Wireless Media:** Wireless transmission employs radio waves, microwaves, or infrared signals to transmit data without physical cables. Technologies like Wi-Fi, Bluetooth, and cellular networks enable mobile and flexible connectivity. Wireless media is advantageous for reducing installation costs and providing access in hard-to-reach areas but can be susceptible to interference and security vulnerabilities (Figure 6.7).

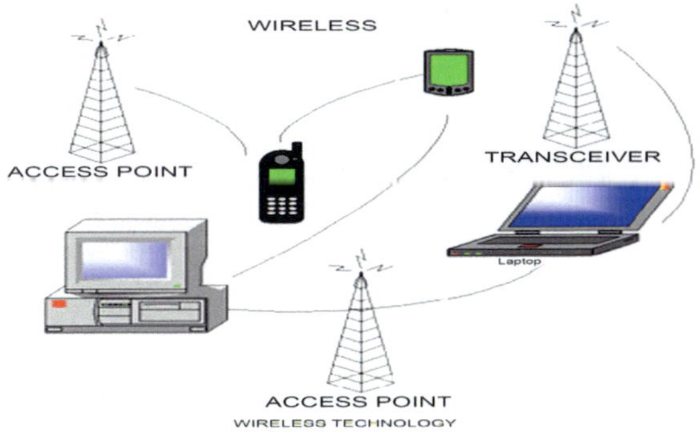

Figure 6.7. Wireless transmissions.

4. **Satellite Communication:** Satellite links are used for long-distance data transmission and remote area connectivity. They can cover vast areas but often experience latency due to the distance signals must travel (Figure 6.8).

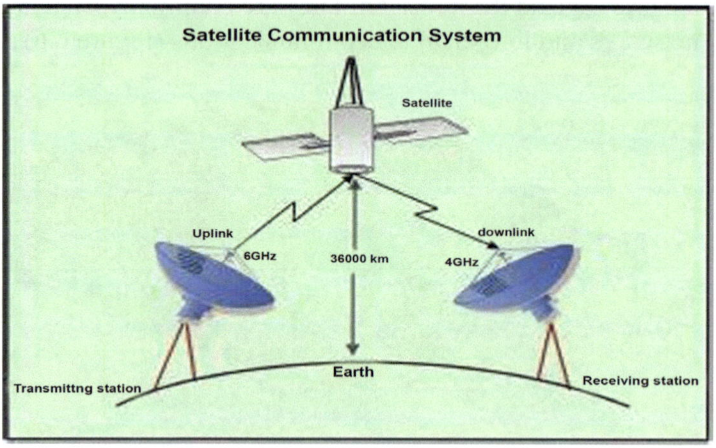

Figure 6.8. Satellite communication system.

Understanding these transmission media helps in selecting the appropriate technology for specific network requirements, ensuring efficient and reliable communication.

6.1.2. Background: Protocol Layers

Protocol layers are an essential concept in networking, structuring communication processes to facilitate data exchange between devices. The layered approach simplifies network design, enhances interoperability, and allows for easier troubleshooting. The most widely referenced model is the OSI (Open Systems Interconnection) model, which comprises seven layers (Figure 6.9):

Figure 6.9. Open systems interconnection (OSI) model.

1. **Physical Layer:** This layer deals with the physical connection between devices. It encompasses the hardware aspects of networking, including cables, switches, and the electrical or optical signals used for data transmission. The physical layer ensures that data bits are transmitted over the medium.
2. **Data Link Layer:** This provides node-to-node data transfer and error detection/correction. It packages raw data from the physical layer into frames and manages protocols for accessing the physical medium. Common protocols at this layer include Ethernet and Wi-Fi.
3. **Network Layer:** Responsible for packet forwarding and routing, the network layer determines the best path for data to travel across multiple networks. It uses logical addressing (IP addresses) to facilitate communication between devices on different networks.
4. **Transport Layer:** This layer ensures reliable data transmission between devices. It segments data into smaller packets and manages flow control, error detection, and recovery. Protocols like TCP (Transmission Control Protocol) and UDP (User Datagram Protocol) operate at this layer, with TCP providing reliability and error correction, while UDP offers faster, connectionless communication.
5. **Session Layer:** This layer establishes, manages, and terminates connections between applications. It coordinates communication sessions and controls the dialog between systems, ensuring that data exchange is synchronized.
6. **Presentation Layer:** This layer formats and translates data for the application layer. It handles data encryption, compression, and translation between different data formats, ensuring that applications can understand each other.
7. **Application Layer:** The topmost layer interacts directly with end-user applications. It provides network services to applications, facilitating functionalities like email, file transfer, and web browsing through protocols such as HTTP, FTP, and SMTP.

This layered architecture promotes modularity, allowing developers to focus on specific layers without affecting others, ultimately enhancing network functionality and scalability.

6.1.3. Background: Addressing and Routing

Addressing and routing are fundamental concepts in networking that enable devices to communicate effectively over networks, ensuring data reaches its intended destination.

- Addressing: This involves assigning unique identifiers to devices on a network. In IP networking, this is achieved through IP addresses, which can be classified as IPv4 or IPv6 (Figure 6.10).

  i. **IPv4:** Consists of 32-bit addresses, typically represented in decimal format (e.g., 192.168.1.1). IPv4 can support approximately 4.3 billion addresses, but due to the rapid growth of the internet, the availability of IPv4 addresses is limited.

  ii. **IPv6:** Introduced to overcome the limitations of IPv4, IPv6 uses 128-bit addresses, allowing for an almost limitless number of unique addresses. IPv6 addresses are represented in hexadecimal format, such as 2001:0db8:85a3:0000:0000:8a2e:0370:7334.

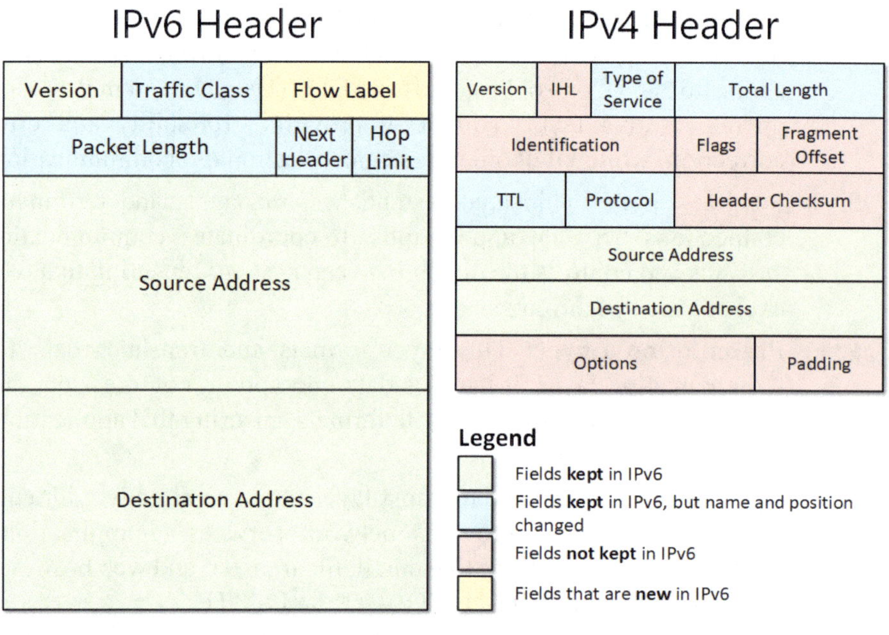

Figure 6.10. IPv6 header vs. IPv4 header.

Each device on a network needs a unique address to send and receive data accurately. Additionally, subnets are used to group devices within a larger network, enhancing organization and efficiency.

- Routing: It is the process of determining the best path for data packets to travel from the source to the destination across interconnected networks. Routers are specialized devices that perform this function by examining the destination IP address in incoming packets and using routing tables to decide the optimal path.

Routing can be categorized into:

i. **Static Routing:** Routes are manually configured and do not change unless updated by a network administrator. This is simpler but less flexible.

ii. **Dynamic Routing:** Routers automatically adjust routes based on current network conditions using protocols like OSPF (Open Shortest Path First) and BGP (Border Gateway Protocol). Dynamic routing allows for more efficient and resilient network operation (Figure 6.11).

Static Routing	Dynamic Routing
Static routing is ideal for small networks	Dynamic routing is suitable for large networks
Configuring static routes involve less cost and can be easily maintained by the network administrator.	Dynamic routing involves cost in terms of CPU processes and bandwidth on the network links.
Routes cannot be changed, until authorized by the network administrator.	Routing protocols find the routes for traversing the packets.
Routers are not updated dynamically in the routing table and hence cannot detect inactive routes.	Routing protocols update the routing table with the updates routes.

Figure 6.11. Static vs. dynamic routing.

Together, addressing and routing ensure that data is directed efficiently across complex networks, facilitating reliable communication in today's interconnected world.

6.2. THREATS TO NETWORK COMMUNICATIONS

Network communications face various threats that can compromise data integrity, confidentiality, and availability. Understanding these threats is essential for implementing effective security measures.

1. Malware: Malicious software, including viruses, worms, Trojans, and ransomware, can infiltrate networks, disrupt services, and steal sensitive information. Ransomware, in particular, encrypts files and demands payment for their release, posing significant risks to businesses and individuals.
2. Phishing: These attacks deceive users into revealing personal information, such as passwords or credit card details, by posing as trustworthy entities. These attacks often occur through deceptive

emails or fake websites, leading to unauthorized access to accounts and data breaches.

3. Man-in-the-Middle (MitM) Attacks: These attacks, an attacker intercepts and alters communications between two parties without their knowledge. This can occur over insecure Wi-Fi networks, where attackers can eavesdrop on data exchanges or manipulate messages, leading to data theft or manipulation.
4. Denial of Service (DoS) Attacks: These attacks overwhelm a network or server with excessive traffic, rendering it unavailable to legitimate users. Distributed Denial of Service (DDoS) attacks amplify this effect by using multiple compromised devices to flood the target with requests, causing significant downtime.
5. Intrusion: Unauthorized access to a network can occur through vulnerabilities in software, weak passwords, or social engineering tactics. Once inside, attackers can exfiltrate data, install additional malware, or disrupt services.
6. Data Breaches: These involve unauthorized access to sensitive data, often resulting from exploited vulnerabilities or insider threats. Breached data can lead to financial loss, reputational damage, and regulatory penalties.
7. Social Engineering: This tactic manipulates individuals into divulging confidential information or performing actions that compromise security. Techniques include pretexting, baiting, and tailgating.

To protect against these threats, organizations should implement robust security measures, including firewalls, intrusion detection systems, employee training, and regular security audits, creating a comprehensive defense strategy for network communications.

6.2.1. Interception: Eavesdropping and Wiretapping

Interception refers to unauthorized monitoring or capturing of data during transmission, often manifesting through eavesdropping and wiretapping. Both methods pose significant threats to privacy and security in communication networks.

- Eavesdropping: It is the act of secretly listening to or monitoring private communications without the consent of the parties involved. It can occur in various forms, including:
  - i. **Passive Eavesdropping:** This involves silently capturing data packets as they travel over a network. Attackers might use

network sniffers or packet analyzers to intercept unencrypted traffic, gaining access to sensitive information such as login credentials, financial data, and personal messages.

ii. **Active Eavesdropping:** In this scenario, the attacker not only listens but may also manipulate the communication. This could involve techniques like session hijacking, where an attacker takes control of an active communication session.

- Wiretapping: This involves intercepting telephone or data communications through physical or electronic means. It can be categorized into:

i. **Traditional Wiretapping:** This method involves physically accessing telephone lines or networks to capture conversations. Law enforcement may conduct this with a warrant, but unauthorized wiretapping is illegal and unethical.

ii. **Digital Wiretapping:** As communications have shifted to digital platforms, wiretapping now includes intercepting VoIP calls, emails, and data transfers. Attackers may exploit vulnerabilities in protocols or use malware to gain access to data streams.

Both eavesdropping and wiretapping can lead to severe consequences, including identity theft, corporate espionage, and privacy violations. To protect against these threats, organizations and individuals should implement strong encryption methods, secure communication protocols, and regular security audits. Awareness and education about the risks associated with interception techniques are also crucial in fostering a culture of security.

6.2.2. Modification, Fabrication: Data Corruption

Modification and fabrication refer to unauthorized changes to data during transmission or storage, leading to data corruption. These threats can severely impact the integrity, authenticity, and reliability of information, posing significant risks to organizations and individuals.

- Modification: Data modification occurs when an unauthorized party alters legitimate data before it reaches its intended destination. This can happen through various means, such as:

i. **Man-in-the-Middle (MitM) Attacks:** In MitM scenarios, attackers intercept communication between two parties and modify the data being exchanged. This could involve changing transaction amounts, tampering with messages, or altering files, leading to misinformation or financial loss.

ii. **Malware:** Certain types of malwares, such as ransomware or Trojans, can modify files and data on infected systems. This can corrupt essential information, render files unusable, or even change critical system settings.

- Fabrication: Data fabrication involves the creation of false data that appears legitimate. This can have far-reaching consequences, such as:

i. **Fake Transactions:** Attackers may generate fraudulent transactions to siphon funds or create misleading records in databases. This can be particularly damaging in financial sectors, where trust in data integrity is paramount.

ii. **False Reports:** Fabricated data can lead to inaccurate reporting, affecting decision-making processes in organizations. For instance, manipulated performance metrics can mislead management, resulting in poor business strategies.

- Consequences and Mitigation: Data corruption due to modification and fabrication can lead to significant financial loss, reputational damage, and legal consequences. To combat these threats, organizations should implement robust security measures, such as:

i. **Data Integrity Checks:** Techniques like checksums and hashes help verify that data remains unaltered during transmission.

ii. **Encryption:** Encrypting data ensures that even if intercepted, it cannot be modified or fabricated without detection.

iii. **Access Controls:** Limiting who can modify data reduces the risk of unauthorized changes.

Awareness and training are also critical in maintaining data integrity and preventing corruption.

6.2.3. Interruption: Loss of Service

Interruption refers to a disruption in network services, which can significantly affect operational continuity and data accessibility. This loss of service can stem from various causes, leading to downtime that impacts both users and organizations.

- Causes of Interruption:

i. **Denial of Service (DoS) Attacks:** These attacks overwhelm a network, server, or service with excessive traffic, rendering it inaccessible to legitimate users. Distributed Denial of Service

(DDoS) attacks amplify this effect by utilizing multiple compromised devices to flood a target with requests, causing significant outages.

ii. **Hardware Failures:** Network components such as routers, switches, and servers can fail due to various reasons, including power outages, overheating, or physical damage. Such failures can interrupt service and require immediate attention to restore functionality.

iii. **Software Issues:** Bugs, configuration errors, or software incompatibilities can lead to system crashes or application failures. Regular updates and patch management are essential to minimize these risks.

iv. **Natural Disasters:** Events like earthquakes, floods, or fires can physically damage infrastructure, resulting in loss of connectivity. Organizations must have disaster recovery plans in place to mitigate these risks.

v. **Human Error:** Mistakes made during system configuration, updates, or maintenance can lead to service interruptions. This can include accidentally disabling services or misconfiguration security settings.

- Consequences of Interruption: The loss of service can lead to significant consequences, including:

i. **Financial Loss:** Downtime can result in lost revenue, especially for e-commerce platforms or critical services.

ii. **Reputational Damage:** Frequent interruptions can erode customer trust and damage an organization's reputation.

iii. **Data Loss:** In some cases, interruptions can lead to data corruption or loss, impacting business continuity.

- Mitigation Strategies: To minimize the risk of service interruption, organizations should implement robust network monitoring, redundancy measures (like failover systems), and disaster recovery plans. Regular training and awareness programs can also help reduce the likelihood of human error, ensuring more resilient network operations.

6.2.4. Port Scanning

Port scanning is a technique used to identify open ports and services on a networked device. It plays a crucial role in network security assessments and penetration testing, helping administrators recognize vulnerabilities and unauthorized services that could be exploited by attackers.

- How Port Scanning Works?: Port scanning involves sending packets to specific ports on a target device and analyzing the responses. Each port corresponds to a different service or application, and they can be in one of three states:
    - i. **Open:** The port is accepting connections, indicating that a service is running.
    - ii. **Closed:** The port is not accepting connections, either because no service is running or it is configured to block access.
    - iii. **Filtered:** The port is blocked by a firewall or other security mechanism, preventing response to scanning attempts.
- Types of Port Scanning Techniques:
    - i. **TCP Connect Scan**: This method establishes a full TCP connection to the target port. If the connection succeeds, the port is open; if it fails, the port is closed.
    - ii. **SYN Scan**: Also known as a half-open scan, it sends SYN packets to the target ports. An open port responds with a SYN-ACK, while a closed port replies with an RST packet. This method is stealthier and less likely to be logged.
    - iii. **UDP Scan**: Since UDP is connectionless, this scan sends UDP packets to ports and waits for a response. Lack of response may indicate an open port, while an ICMP "port unreachable" message indicates a closed port.
- Ethical Considerations: While port scanning can be a valuable tool for identifying vulnerabilities, it can also be perceived as malicious activity, especially if performed without authorization. Organizations should conduct scans as part of a legitimate security assessment, ensuring compliance with legal and ethical standards. Regular port scanning helps maintain a secure network environment by proactively identifying and addressing vulnerabilities before they can be exploited.

6.2.5. Vulnerability Summary

A vulnerability summary provides an overview of potential weaknesses in a system, application, or network that could be exploited by attackers to gain unauthorized access or disrupt services. Identifying and addressing these vulnerabilities is crucial for maintaining cybersecurity and protecting sensitive data.

- Types of Vulnerabilities:
    i. **Software Vulnerabilities:** Flaws or bugs in software applications can be exploited by attackers. This includes buffer overflows, improper input validation, and outdated software lacking patches. Regular updates and patch management are essential to mitigate these risks.
    ii. **Network Vulnerabilities:** Weaknesses in network configurations, such as open ports, misconfigured firewalls, or insecure wireless networks, can expose systems to attacks. Tools like port scanning can help identify these vulnerabilities, enabling organizations to strengthen their defenses.
    iii. **Authentication Vulnerabilities:** Weak or poorly implemented authentication mechanisms, such as inadequate password policies or lack of multi-factor authentication, can allow unauthorized users to access systems. Implementing strong authentication practices is critical to safeguarding sensitive information.
    iv. **Configuration Vulnerabilities:** Default configurations, especially in web servers and database management systems, can leave systems open to attack. Organizations should regularly review and harden configurations to align with security best practices.
    v. **Social Engineering Vulnerabilities:** Human factors often represent the weakest link in security. Phishing attacks and other social engineering tactics can trick users into revealing credentials or executing harmful actions. Regular training and awareness programs can help mitigate this risk.
- Importance of Vulnerability Management: A robust vulnerability management program involves regular assessments, continuous monitoring, and timely remediation of identified vulnerabilities. Organizations should conduct vulnerability scans, penetration testing, and risk assessments to proactively address weaknesses.

By maintaining an updated vulnerability summary and implementing comprehensive security measures, organizations can significantly reduce the risk of successful attacks, ensuring the confidentiality, integrity, and availability of their data and systems.

6.3. WIRELESS NETWORK SECURITY

Wireless network security is critical for protecting data transmitted over wireless connections, which are inherently more vulnerable to interception and attacks compared to wired networks. Ensuring the security of wireless networks involves several key practices and technologies.

- Security Protocols:
  i. **WPA3:** The latest Wi-Fi Protected Access (WPA) protocol, WPA3, enhances security through improved encryption and protection against brute-force attacks. It replaces WPA2, which, while widely used, has known vulnerabilities.
  ii. **WEP:** Wired Equivalent Privacy (WEP) was one of the first security protocols for wireless networks but is now considered outdated and insecure. Organizations should avoid using WEP due to its easily exploitable weaknesses.
  iii. **WPA2:** While more secure than WEP, WPA2 has vulnerabilities that can be exploited, such as the KRACK attack. Organizations should aim to upgrade to WPA3 where possible.
- Practices:
  i. **Strong Passwords:** Implementing strong, complex passwords for Wi-Fi networks is essential. Regularly updating passwords and using passphrases can help prevent unauthorized access.
  ii. **Network Segmentation:** Separating guest networks from internal networks limits exposure to sensitive data. This ensures that visitors cannot access critical resources.
  iii. **Encryption:** Always use strong encryption for data transmission. WPA2 and WPA3 provide robust encryption standards that help protect data as it travels over the air.
  iv. **Regular Updates:** Keeping routers and access points updated with the latest firmware helps protect against known vulnerabilities.
  v. **Disable Broadcasting:** Hiding the SSID (Service Set Identifier) can deter casual users from attempting to connect to the network, though it does not provide full security.
  vi. **Intrusion Detection:** Implementing systems to monitor network activity can help identify and respond to unauthorized access attempts.

Wireless network security is essential in today's mobile and interconnected world. By employing strong security protocols, best practices, and ongoing monitoring, organizations can significantly reduce the risks associated with wireless communication and protect sensitive information from potential threats.

6.3.1. Wi-Fi Background

Wi-Fi, short for Wireless Fidelity, is a technology that allows electronic devices to connect to a local area network (LAN) wirelessly. It utilizes radio waves to transmit data, enabling devices such as smartphones, laptops, tablets, and smart home devices to communicate with routers and access points without the need for physical cables.

- Development and Standards: The development of Wi-Fi began in the late 1990s, with the introduction of the IEEE 802.11 standards by the Institute of Electrical and Electronics Engineers (IEEE). The first standard, 802.11, was released in 1997, offering data rates of up to 2 Mbps. Subsequent standards have improved speed, range, and security:
  - i. **802.11b (1999):** Increased speeds up to 11 Mbps and operated on the 2.4 GHz frequency band.
  - ii. **802.11g (2003):** Combined the best features of 802.11b and provided speeds up to 54 Mbps, also on the 2.4 GHz band.
  - iii. **802.11n (2009):** Introduced multiple-input and multiple-output (MIMO) technology, allowing for greater speeds (up to 600 Mbps) and improved range by using multiple antennas.
  - iv. **802.11ac (2013):** Operated on the 5 GHz band, offering speeds exceeding 1 Gbps and better performance in crowded environments.
  - v. **802.11ax (Wi-Fi 6, 2019):** Further enhanced performance, enabling higher data rates, increased capacity, and better efficiency in environments with many connected devices.
- Applications: Wi-Fi technology is widely used in homes, businesses, and public spaces to facilitate internet access and enable communication between devices. It supports various applications, from basic web browsing and streaming to IoT devices that control home automation systems.

Wi-Fi has revolutionized how we connect and communicate, providing flexibility and convenience in our increasingly digital lives. Its continuous evolution and the introduction of newer standards promise to enhance connectivity and performance further, adapting to the growing demands of users worldwide.

6.3.2. Vulnerabilities in Wireless Networks

Wireless networks, while offering flexibility and convenience, are inherently vulnerable to various security threats. Understanding these vulnerabilities is essential for implementing effective protective measures.

- Common Vulnerabilities:
  i. **Weak Encryption Protocols:** Older encryption methods like WEP (Wired Equivalent Privacy) have known weaknesses that can be easily exploited. Although WPA (Wi-Fi Protected Access) and WPA2 improved security, they are not immune to attacks. WPA3 is more secure, but not all devices support it.
  ii. **Unauthorized Access:** Wireless networks can be susceptible to unauthorized users accessing the network if proper security measures are not in place. Default settings on routers, including default passwords and SSIDs, can provide an easy entry point for attackers.
  iii. **Eavesdropping:** Since wireless signals are broadcast through the air, they can be intercepted by anyone within range. Attackers can use packet sniffers to capture sensitive information, such as passwords and personal data, if encryption is weak or absent.
  iv. **Rogue Access Points:** Attackers may set up rogue access points that mimic legitimate networks. Unsuspecting users may connect to these malicious networks, allowing attackers to capture data or launch attacks.
  v. **Denial of Service (DoS) Attacks:** Wireless networks can be targeted with DoS attacks, overwhelming the network with traffic and rendering it unavailable to legitimate users. This can disrupt business operations and accessibility.
  vi. **Signal Interference:** Physical obstructions and electronic devices can interfere with Wi-Fi signals, leading to connectivity issues. This can be exploited by attackers to cause disruptions.
- Mitigation Strategies: To mitigate these vulnerabilities, organizations should implement strong encryption (preferably WPA3), regularly update firmware, and use complex passwords. Network segmentation, disabling SSID broadcasting, and employing intrusion detection systems can further enhance security. Regular

security assessments and employee training on safe practices are also essential in maintaining a secure wireless environment.

6.3.3. Failed Countermeasure: Wired Equivalent Privacy (WEP)

WEP (Wired Equivalent Privacy) was introduced in 1997 as part of the IEEE 802.11 standard to provide a level of security comparable to wired networks. However, it has proven to be fundamentally flawed and is now considered ineffective for protecting wireless communications.

- Vulnerabilities of WEP:
  - **i. Weak Encryption:** WEP uses a 40-bit key for encryption, which can be easily cracked through brute-force attacks. Even with the 104-bit extension, the encryption strength remains inadequate by today's standards. Tools like Aircrack-ng can decrypt WEP-protected traffic in a matter of minutes.
  - **ii. Static Keys:** WEP relies on static encryption keys that remain unchanged during a session. If an attacker can capture enough data packets, they can perform statistical analysis to recover the key. Once compromised, the entire network becomes vulnerable.
  - **iii. Initialization Vector (IV) Issues:** WEP uses an initialization vector (IV) to randomize the encryption process. However, the IV is relatively short (24 bits), leading to frequent repetitions. This results in predictable patterns that attackers can exploit, allowing for easy decryption.
  - **iv. No Authentication:** While WEP provides encryption, it lacks robust authentication mechanisms. It relies on shared keys, which means anyone who knows the key can access the network, leading to potential unauthorized access.
- Legacy and Impact: Due to these vulnerabilities, WEP has been largely abandoned in favor of more secure protocols like WPA (Wi-Fi protected access) and WPA2, which offer improved encryption and authentication methods. Despite its initial intent to secure wireless communications, WEP's weaknesses have made it a cautionary tale in network security, highlighting the necessity for continuous evolution in security measures to counter emerging threats.

WEP's failure serves as a reminder of the importance of adopting robust security protocols and regularly updating them to defend against evolving cyber threats.

Organizations should avoid using WEP and transition to stronger encryption methods to safeguard their wireless networks effectively.

6.3.4. Stronger Protocol Suite: WPA (Wi-Fi Protected Access)

Wi-Fi protected access (WPA) was introduced in 2003 as a more secure alternative to WEP (Wired Equivalent Privacy). Developed in response to the vulnerabilities inherent in WEP, WPA enhances wireless security through robust encryption and improved authentication mechanisms.

- Key Features of WPA:
    - i. **Improved Encryption:** WPA utilizes the Temporal Key Integrity Protocol (TKIP), which dynamically generates a new key for each data packet transmitted over the network. This approach mitigates the risks associated with static keys used in WEP, making it significantly harder for attackers to decrypt data.
    - ii. **Message Integrity Check:** WPA includes a Message Integrity Code (MIC) to verify the integrity of transmitted data. This helps ensure that packets are not altered in transit, protecting against man-in-the-middle (MitM) attacks and replay attacks.
    - iii. **Authentication Methods:** WPA supports multiple authentication methods, including pre-shared keys (PSK) for home networks and 802.1X authentication for enterprise environments. This flexibility allows organizations to implement stronger authentication measures based on their specific needs.
    - iv. **Backward Compatibility:** WPA was designed to be compatible with existing hardware using WEP, enabling a smoother transition for users and organizations upgrading their security without the need for new equipment.
- Transition to WPA2: In 2004, WPA2 was introduced as an enhancement of WPA, incorporating the Advanced Encryption Standard (AES) for even stronger encryption. WPA2 mandates the use of AES, providing a higher level of security and making it the current standard for wireless networks.

WPA and its successor, WPA2, have become essential for securing wireless networks, addressing the vulnerabilities that plagued WEP. By implementing WPA, organizations can significantly improve their wireless security posture, safeguard sensitive data and enhancing overall network integrity. As wireless technologies continue to evolve, ongoing adoption of robust security protocols remains critical to counter emerging threats.

6.4. DENIAL OF SERVICE

A denial of service (DoS) attack aims to make a network service unavailable to its intended users by overwhelming it with excessive traffic or exploiting vulnerabilities that disrupt service functionality. These attacks can significantly impact businesses, government services, and individuals, leading to financial loss and reputational damage.

- Types of Denial-of-Service Attacks:
  - i. **Volume-based Attacks:** These involve flooding the target with high levels of traffic, exceeding its bandwidth capacity. Common methods include ICMP floods (ping floods) and UDP floods. The goal is to saturate the network, making it impossible for legitimate traffic to reach the server.
  - ii. **Protocol Attacks:** These exploit weaknesses in network protocols to consume server resources. Examples include SYN floods, which send numerous SYN requests to a server without completing the handshake, and fragmented packet attacks that overload the server's ability to reassemble packets.
  - iii. **Application Layer Attacks:** These target specific applications by sending requests designed to exhaust resources. For example, an HTTP flood attack sends many legitimate-looking requests to a web server, overwhelming it and causing legitimate requests to be dropped.
- Distributed Denial of Service (DDoS): These attacks amplify the impact of DoS attacks by using multiple compromised devices (botnets) to launch coordinated assaults from various sources. This makes detection and mitigation more challenging since the traffic appears to come from numerous legitimate users.
- Mitigation Strategies: To defend against DoS and DDoS attacks, organizations can employ several strategies:
  - i. **Traffic Filtering:** Implementing firewalls and intrusion detection systems to filter malicious traffic can help mitigate attacks.
  - ii. **Rate Limiting**: Controlling the amount of traffic sent to servers can prevent them from being overwhelmed.
  - iii. **Redundancy and Load Balancing**: Distributing traffic across multiple servers can help maintain service availability even during an attack.

Denial of service attacks pose significant threats to network reliability and security. By understanding their nature and implementing robust mitigation strategies, organizations can protect their services from these disruptive events.

6.4.1. Example: Massive Estonian Web Failure

The massive web failure in Estonia in April 2007 serves as a significant example of a Denial of Service (DoS) attack, illustrating the potential impact of cyber warfare on a nation's infrastructure. This incident was triggered by political tensions surrounding the relocation of a Soviet war memorial in Tallinn, leading to a wave of online protests.

- Attack Overview: In late April 2007, Estonia experienced a series of coordinated DDoS attacks targeting various websites, including government portals, banks, and media outlets. The attacks aimed to disrupt services and create chaos, overwhelming these sites with traffic generated from thousands of compromised computers around the world, forming a botnet.
- Impact: The scale of the attacks was unprecedented, affecting not only government websites but also the online banking systems of major financial institutions, making it nearly impossible for citizens to access their accounts or conduct transactions. Key services, including telecommunications and emergency response systems, faced disruptions, demonstrating the attack's broad-reaching effects on national infrastructure.
- Response and Aftermath: In response to the attacks, Estonia's government worked closely with international cybersecurity experts and organizations to mitigate the ongoing threat. They implemented various countermeasures, including enhanced traffic filtering and the deployment of additional security protocols. The incident highlighted the importance of cybersecurity and the need for countries to prepare for potential cyber warfare.

The Estonian web failure stands as a cautionary tale about the vulnerabilities of digital infrastructures in an increasingly interconnected world. It underscores the necessity for robust cybersecurity measures and international collaboration to defend against future threats. This event marked a turning point, prompting many nations to reevaluate their cybersecurity strategies and preparedness in the face of similar attacks.

6.4.2. How Service Is Denied?

Denial of service (DoS) attacks aim to make a network service unavailable to its intended users, effectively disrupting normal operations. This can be achieved through various methods, each designed to overwhelm systems, exhaust resources, or exploit vulnerabilities.

1. Traffic Overload: One of the most common ways services is denied is by overwhelming a server or network with excessive traffic. Attackers can flood the target with numerous requests, consuming its bandwidth and processing power. This can include:
   - **i.** **ICMP Floods**: These send a high volume of ping requests, leading to network congestion.
   - **ii.** **UDP Floods**: By sending large numbers of User Datagram Protocol packets to random ports, the server becomes overloaded as it attempts to respond to each request.
2. Resource Exhaustion: Certain attacks focus on exhausting specific server resources:
   - **i.** **SYN Flood:** This technique sends a barrage of SYN requests (part of the TCP handshake) without completing the connection. The server allocates resources for these half-open connections, eventually exhausting its capacity.
   - **ii.** **HTTP Flood:** By sending seemingly legitimate HTTP requests, attackers can exhaust the server's ability to handle legitimate traffic, causing slowdowns or crashes.
3. Exploiting Vulnerabilities: Some attacks target specific weaknesses in software or network protocols:
   - **i.** **Application Layer Attacks:** These exploit weaknesses in applications (e.g., web servers) to consume resources, causing them to slow down or become unresponsive.
   - **ii.** **Fragmentation Attacks:** By sending fragmented packets, attackers can force servers to expend excessive resources on reassembly, leading to denial of service.

The primary objective of a DoS attack is to disrupt the availability of a service, causing inconvenience, financial loss, and damage to reputation. Organizations must implement robust security measures, including traffic monitoring, filtering, and redundancy, to protect against these disruptive tactics and ensure service continuity.

6.4.3. Flooding Attacks in Detail

Flooding attacks are a type of Denial of Service (DoS) attack where the attacker overwhelms a target such as a server, network, or application with an excessive amount of traffic or requests. The goal is to consume resources and render the target unresponsive to legitimate users. Here are some common types of flooding attacks:

1. SYN Flood: In a SYN flood, an attacker exploits the TCP handshake process. The attacker sends a flood of SYN requests (the first step in establishing a TCP connection) to a target server without completing the handshake. The server allocates resources for these half-open connections, leading to exhaustion of memory and processing capacity, ultimately preventing legitimate users from establishing connections.
2. UDP Flood: A UDP flood involves sending a large number of User Datagram Protocol (UDP) packets to random ports on the target system. The server, upon receiving these packets, will respond with ICMP "port unreachable" messages for closed ports. This flood of incoming packets can saturate the target's bandwidth and processing power, disrupting normal operations.
3. ICMP Flood: ICMP (Internet Control Message Protocol) floods, commonly known as ping floods, send a high volume of ICMP echo request packets (ping requests) to the target. The server, attempting to respond to these requests, can become overwhelmed, leading to network congestion and potential service interruption.
4. HTTP Flood: HTTP floods target web servers by sending a massive number of HTTP requests, often mimicking legitimate traffic. This can exhaust server resources, making it difficult for genuine users to access the website.

- Mitigation Strategies: To defend against flooding attacks, organizations can implement rate limiting, which controls the number of requests accepted from a single IP address. Firewalls and intrusion detection systems can also be configured to identify and block malicious traffic patterns. Additionally, employing Content Delivery Networks (CDNs) can help absorb excess traffic and maintain service availability during an attack.

Flooding attacks pose significant risks to network and service availability. Understanding their mechanics and implementing robust defenses is crucial for maintaining operational integrity.

6.4.4. Network Flooding Caused by Malicious Code

Network flooding caused by malicious code involves the deliberate use of malware to overwhelm a network's resources, leading to service disruption and potential data breaches. This type of attack can manifest in various forms, primarily targeting network infrastructure, servers, and devices.

- Mechanisms of Malicious Code Flooding:
  i. **Botnets:** One of the most common methods involves creating a botnet—a network of compromised devices controlled by an attacker. These bots can be instructed to generate massive amounts of traffic to a target, making it difficult for the target to handle legitimate requests. Botnets often consist of Internet of Things (IoT) devices, which are frequently less secure and more susceptible to compromise.

  ii. **DDoS Attacks:** Distributed denial of service (DDoS) attacks utilize botnets to execute coordinated flooding attacks. Attackers can deploy various techniques, such as SYN floods or UDP floods, to inundate the target with traffic. The sheer volume can incapacitate servers and networks, leading to significant downtime.

  iii. **Malware Deployment:** Malicious code can be embedded in software or delivered through phishing emails, prompting users to inadvertently install it. Once active, this malware may execute flooding attacks on local networks, consuming bandwidth and resources.

  iv. **Resource Exploitation:** Some malware is designed to exploit specific vulnerabilities in applications or network protocols, enabling it to generate excessive requests that deplete server resources or bandwidth.

- Mitigation Strategies: To counteract network flooding from malicious code, organizations should implement several strategies:
  i. **Firewalls and Intrusion Detection Systems**: These tools can help identify and block malicious traffic patterns, preventing flooding before it affects the network.

  ii. **Regular Software Updates:** Keeping software and systems updated can close vulnerabilities that malware exploits.

  iii. **Traffic Monitoring:** Employing tools to monitor network traffic can help detect unusual patterns indicative of flooding attacks, allowing for timely responses.

Network flooding caused by malicious code poses significant threats to organizational integrity and operational continuity. By understanding these mechanisms and implementing robust defenses, organizations can better protect themselves against such disruptive attacks.

6.4.5. Network Flooding by Resource Exhaustion

Network flooding by resource exhaustion is a type of Denial of Service (DoS) attack that targets a network's resources, overwhelming them to the point of incapacitation. This technique exploits system limitations, such as bandwidth, memory, and processing power, to deny legitimate users access to services.

- Mechanisms of Resource Exhaustion Attacks:
  - i. **SYN Flood Attacks:** In this common attack, an attacker sends a barrage of SYN requests to a server without completing the TCP handshake. The server allocates resources to track these half-open connections, eventually exhausting its capacity to handle legitimate traffic.
  - ii. **UDP Flood Attacks:** By sending numerous User Datagram Protocol (UDP) packets to random ports on a target server, attackers can overwhelm its bandwidth and processing power. The server responds with ICMP "port unreachable" messages for closed ports, further consuming its resources.
  - iii. **HTTP Flood Attacks:** These attacks target web servers by sending an excessive number of HTTP requests. The requests may appear legitimate, making them harder to distinguish from normal traffic. As the server struggles to respond to the flood of requests, it can slow down or become unresponsive.
  - iv. **Application Layer Attacks:** Attackers may exploit specific vulnerabilities in applications to exhaust server resources. For instance, a malicious request designed to trigger excessive processing can lead to resource depletion, impacting availability.
- Mitigation Strategies: To defend against resource exhaustion attacks, organizations can implement several strategies:
  - i. **Rate Limiting:** This technique restricts the number of requests a server will accept from a single IP address within a certain time frame, helping to prevent overload.
  - ii. **Traffic Filtering:** Firewalls and intrusion detection systems can help filter out malicious traffic, preventing it from reaching sensitive network resources.

iii. **Load Balancing:** Distributing incoming traffic across multiple servers can help maintain service availability during an attack.

Network flooding by resource exhaustion poses significant risks to system availability and performance. Understanding the mechanisms behind these attacks and implementing robust defenses is crucial for maintaining operational integrity and safeguarding resources.

6.4.6. Denial of Service by Addressing Failures

Denial of Service (DoS) attacks can also occur due to addressing failures, which exploit weaknesses in how network devices handle IP addressing and routing. These failures can prevent legitimate traffic from reaching its intended destination, effectively disrupting services and rendering them unavailable.

- Mechanisms of Addressing Failures:

i. **IP Spoofing:** Attackers can forge the source IP address of packets, making it appear as though the traffic is coming from a legitimate source. This can overwhelm a target by flooding it with traffic that seems authentic but is actually malicious. Spoofed packets can also lead to confusion in routing, further complicating the network's ability to manage incoming requests.

ii. **Route Injection Attacks:** Attackers may manipulate routing tables to redirect traffic away from legitimate servers. By injecting incorrect routing information, they can cause legitimate users to be unable to reach the intended destination, effectively denying service.

iii. **Address Resolution Protocol (ARP) Spoofing:** In local networks, attackers can use ARP spoofing to associate their MAC address with the IP address of a legitimate device. This can redirect traffic intended for the legitimate device to the attacker, disrupting communications and causing service interruptions.

iv. **Subnet Overload:** Attackers can exploit subnet addressing by flooding a specific subnet with traffic. If the subnet is overwhelmed, it can affect all devices within that range, leading to a denial of service for legitimate users.

- Mitigation Strategies: To combat addressing failures, organizations can implement several strategies:

i. **Ingress and Egress Filtering**: Configuring routers to filter incoming and outgoing traffic can help prevent IP spoofing and ensure that only legitimate packets enter or leave the network.

ii. **Routing Protocol Security**: Using secure routing protocols and implementing authentication measures can help prevent route injection attacks.

iii. **ARP Security Measures**: Employing ARP security techniques, such as Dynamic ARP Inspection, can mitigate ARP spoofing risks.

Denial of Service attacks leveraging addressing failures pose serious risks to network integrity and availability. By understanding these vulnerabilities and implementing robust security measures, organizations can better protect their networks from such disruptive incidents.

6.4.7. Traffic Redirection

Traffic redirection is a crucial technique in web management and digital marketing that involves directing users from one URL to another. This process can enhance user experience, improve SEO rankings, and maintain website integrity during changes.

There are several methods for traffic redirection, with the most common being 301 and 302 redirects. A 301 redirect is a permanent redirect, signaling to search engines that a page has moved permanently. This method helps preserve SEO rankings, ensuring that the link equity from the old URL is transferred to the new one. It's often used during site migrations, rebranding, or when content is moved to a different domain.

In contrast, a 302 redirect is temporary, indicating that the original URL will return. This is useful for situations like A/B testing or when content is temporarily relocated. Using a 302 redirect can prevent search engines from indexing the temporary URL, preserving the original page's SEO value.

Redirection can also be implemented at different levels, such as server-side redirects, which are executed on the server before the content reaches the user, and client-side redirects, which are handled by the user's browser. The choice between these methods depends on specific use cases and desired outcomes.

Proper implementation of traffic redirection is essential to avoid issues like broken links or poor user experience. Additionally, excessive or improper redirection can lead to slower page load times, negatively impacting SEO and user satisfaction. Therefore, it's important to use redirection judiciously, ensuring it serves a clear purpose and is optimized for both users and search engines. Overall, traffic redirection is a vital tool for effective web management and online marketing strategies.

6.4.8. DNS Attacks

DNS attacks exploit vulnerabilities in the Domain Name System (DNS), which translates user-friendly domain names into IP addresses that computers use to identify each other. These attacks can disrupt services, compromise data integrity, and lead to severe security breaches.

One common type of DNS attack is DNS spoofing (or cache poisoning), where an attacker corrupts the DNS cache of a resolver. By injecting false DNS records, the attacker redirects users to malicious sites without their knowledge. This can lead to phishing attacks, where users unknowingly provide sensitive information to impersonated sites.

Another prevalent attack is the DNS amplification attack, a type of Distributed Denial of Service (DDoS) attack. Here, attackers exploit publicly accessible DNS servers by sending a small query that elicits a much larger response. This flood of traffic can overwhelm a target server, making it unavailable to legitimate users.

Domain hijacking is another threat, where attackers gain unauthorized access to a domain registrar account, allowing them to take control of a domain name. This can lead to loss of business identity and disruption of services.

DNS tunneling is a more sophisticated attack that allows data exfiltration by encoding data in DNS queries and responses. This can help attackers bypass network security measures, making detection difficult.

To mitigate DNS attacks, organizations should implement security measures such as DNSSEC (Domain Name System Security Extensions), which adds a layer of verification to DNS responses. Regular monitoring of DNS records and employing redundant DNS services can also help ensure resilience against attacks.

Overall, understanding and addressing the vulnerabilities of DNS is critical in safeguarding online assets and maintaining service availability in an increasingly digital world.

6.4.9. Exploiting Known Vulnerabilities

Exploiting known vulnerabilities refers to the practice of taking advantage of security flaws in software, hardware, or systems that are publicly documented and often have established methods for exploitation. These vulnerabilities can be found in operating systems, applications, and network protocols, and they pose significant risks to organizations and individuals.

Attackers typically leverage known vulnerabilities to gain unauthorized access, escalate privileges, or disrupt services. Common methods of exploitation include buffer overflows, SQL injection, and cross-site scripting (XSS). For example, a buffer overflow occurs when data exceeds a buffer's storage capacity, allowing attackers to overwrite memory and execute arbitrary code.

One of the primary reasons known vulnerabilities are exploited is the failure to apply security patches. Vendors regularly release updates to fix identified flaws, but organizations may neglect to implement these patches due to downtime concerns or lack of awareness. As a result, systems remain exposed, providing attackers with an opportunity to exploit them.

The widespread availability of vulnerability databases, such as the National Vulnerability Database (NVD) and Common Vulnerabilities and Exposures (CVE), makes it easier for attackers to identify and exploit these weaknesses. Cybercriminals may use automated tools and scripts to scan networks for unpatched vulnerabilities, significantly increasing the risk of a successful attack.

To mitigate the risk of exploitation, organizations should prioritize regular security assessments, patch management, and employee training. Implementing a robust security posture, including firewalls, intrusion detection systems, and vulnerability management programs, can help reduce exposure to known vulnerabilities.

6.4.10. Physical Disconnection

Physical disconnection is a security strategy that involves isolating a system or network from external access to protect sensitive data and critical infrastructure. This method is particularly effective against cyber threats, as it creates a barrier that prevents unauthorized access and mitigates the risk of remote attacks.

One of the most common forms of physical disconnection is the use of air-gapped networks, which are entirely isolated from the internet and other networks. Air-gapping is often employed in highly sensitive environments, such as military installations, financial institutions, and critical infrastructure sectors. By ensuring that systems are not connected to external networks, organizations can safeguard against threats like malware, ransomware, and hacking attempts.

However, while physical disconnection offers significant security advantages, it also presents challenges. For instance, the lack of connectivity can hinder communication and collaboration, making it difficult for teams to share information or access cloud-based resources. Additionally, updating software and systems can be more cumbersome, as manual intervention is required to transfer updates or patches physically.

Moreover, physical disconnection does not eliminate all security risks. Insider threats remain a concern, as individuals with physical access to the systems can still exploit vulnerabilities or compromise data. Therefore, organizations must complement physical disconnection with robust access controls, surveillance, and employee training to mitigate these risks.

In conclusion, physical disconnection is a powerful security measure that significantly enhances the protection of sensitive systems and data. By isolating critical infrastructure from external threats, organizations can reduce their vulnerability to cyberattacks while still addressing the associated operational challenges. Proper implementation, alongside a comprehensive security strategy, is essential to maximize the effectiveness of this approach.

6.5. DISTRIBUTED DENIAL-OF-SERVICE

A Distributed Denial-of-Service (DDoS) attack is a malicious attempt to disrupt the normal functioning of a targeted server, service, or network by overwhelming it with a flood of internet traffic. Unlike a standard Denial-of-Service (DoS) attack, which typically involves a single source, DDoS attacks utilize multiple compromised devices—often forming a botnet—to launch a coordinated assault.

The attack process begins with the attacker infecting numerous devices, such as computers, IoT devices, or servers, with malware. Once these devices are under control, the attacker can direct them to send a massive volume of requests to the target. This overwhelming surge of traffic can exhaust the target's resources, rendering it unable to respond to legitimate requests and ultimately causing downtime.

DDoS attacks can take various forms, including volumetric attacks that aim to saturate the bandwidth, protocol attacks that exploit weaknesses in the network protocols, and application layer attacks that target specific applications or services. Each type poses unique challenges and requires different mitigation strategies.

The impact of a DDoS attack can be severe, resulting in significant financial losses, reputational damage, and decreased customer trust. Organizations may face extended downtime, lost revenue, and the costs associated with recovery efforts.

To defend against DDoS attacks, organizations can implement several strategies, including traffic analysis, rate limiting, and the use of DDoS protection services. Employing robust firewalls and intrusion detection systems can help identify and mitigate abnormal traffic patterns before they overwhelm the system.

In conclusion, DDoS attacks represent a significant threat to online services and infrastructure. Understanding their mechanics and implementing proactive defenses is crucial for organizations to safeguard their operations and maintain service availability in the face of these attacks.

6.5.1. Scripted Denial-of-Service Attacks

Scripted Denial-of-Service (DoS) attacks refer to automated attacks that leverage scripts or tools to overwhelm a target server or network, causing disruptions in service. Unlike traditional DoS attacks, which may be initiated manually, scripted attacks use pre-written code to generate high volumes of traffic or requests rapidly, making them more efficient and harder to mitigate.

These attacks typically exploit vulnerabilities in web applications or network protocols. Attackers can use various scripting languages, such as Python or JavaScript, to create bots that send numerous requests or data packets to the target, effectively saturating its resources. Common methods include sending multiple connection requests, exploiting poorly designed APIs, or using scripts that continuously refresh pages, all of which can exhaust server capacity.

One well-known example is the SYN flood attack, where an attacker sends a series of SYN requests to a server but never completes the handshake process, leaving the server with open connections and unable to handle legitimate requests.

The impact of scripted DoS attacks can be significant, leading to website downtime, loss of revenue, and damage to an organization's reputation. Moreover, these attacks can be executed relatively easily, often requiring minimal technical knowledge and utilizing publicly available scripts or tools.

To defend against scripted DoS attacks, organizations should employ several strategies. These include implementing rate limiting to control the number of requests a user can make, using web application firewalls (WAFs) to filter malicious traffic, and employing intrusion detection systems (IDS) to monitor for abnormal activity.

In summary, scripted DoS attacks pose a substantial threat to online services. Understanding their mechanics and implementing robust defense mechanisms is essential for maintaining service availability and protecting against disruptions.

6.5.2. Bots

Bots, short for "robots," are automated software programs designed to perform specific tasks on the internet. They can operate independently or semi-autonomously, executing actions much faster than a human could. While many bots serve beneficial purposes, such as web crawlers for search engines or chatbots for customer service, they can also be used maliciously.

- **Types of Bots:**
  i. **Web Crawlers:** These bots index web pages for search engines like Google, helping users find relevant information quickly.
  ii. **Chatbots:** Used by businesses to handle customer inquiries, chatbots can provide instant support and engage users on websites and messaging platforms.
  iii. **Malicious Bots:** These include bots that perform harmful activities, such as DDoS attacks, scraping data from websites, or conducting fraud. For example, botnets—collections of compromised devices controlled by a single attacker—can launch coordinated attacks to disrupt services or steal sensitive data.
- **Impact of Bots:** Bots can significantly affect online activities. Beneficial bots enhance user experience and improve efficiency, while malicious bots can lead to data breaches, financial loss, and reputational damage. Businesses often struggle to differentiate between legitimate bot traffic and malicious activity, making it essential to implement robust security measures.
- **Mitigation Strategies:** To combat malicious bots, organizations employ various strategies, including:
  i. **Bot Management Tools**: These systems help identify, categorize, and mitigate harmful bot traffic.
  ii. **CAPTCHA**: Challenges like CAPTCHAs can distinguish human users from bots, reducing the likelihood of automated attacks.
  iii. **Rate Limiting**: By controlling the number of requests from a single source, businesses can prevent abuse.

In conclusion, while bots play a crucial role in automating tasks and enhancing online experiences, they also pose significant challenges. Effective management and security measures are vital for harnessing their benefits while mitigating potential threats.

6.5.3. Botnets

A botnet is a network of compromised computers or devices, controlled remotely by a single attacker or group. These networks are created by infecting devices with malware, allowing the attacker to execute commands across all connected devices simultaneously. Botnets can range in size from a few infected machines to millions.

- **Types of Botnets:**
  i. **DDoS Botnets:** These are used to launch Distributed Denial-of-Service attacks, overwhelming a target with traffic to disrupt services.
  ii. **Spam Botnets:** These send out massive volumes of spam emails, often for phishing or advertising malicious products.
  iii. **Credential Theft Botnets:** These aim to harvest login credentials and personal information from users.
- **Impact of Botnets:** Botnets can cause significant harm, including financial losses, data breaches, and reputational damage. They can disrupt essential services and even impact infrastructure by targeting critical systems.
- **Mitigation Strategies:** To defend against botnets, organizations can:
  – Implement robust security measures, such as firewalls and intrusion detection systems.
  – Regularly update software and conduct vulnerability assessments.
  – Use botnet detection tools to identify and mitigate bot traffic.

6.5.4. Malicious Autonomous Mobile Agents

Malicious autonomous mobile agents are self-governing software entities designed to perform tasks on behalf of a user or system but with harmful intent. Unlike traditional software, these agents can move across networks, adapt their behavior, and operate independently, making them particularly dangerous.

- **Characteristics:**
  i. **Autonomy:** They can make decisions without human intervention, allowing them to execute tasks like data theft or system infiltration.
  ii. **Mobility:** These agents can traverse different network nodes, spread malware or extracting information as they go.
  iii. **Adaptability:** Malicious agents can adjust their strategies based on the environment or defenses they encounter, making detection and mitigation challenging.
- **Common Uses:**
  i. **Data Exfiltration**: Stealing sensitive information by navigating through network systems.

ii. **Surveillance**: Monitoring user activities or system vulnerabilities.

iii. **Disruption**: Launching attacks on networks or systems, causing downtime or damage.

- **Impact:** The presence of malicious autonomous mobile agents can lead to significant security breaches, loss of sensitive data, and operational disruptions. Their ability to operate covertly makes them difficult to detect and neutralize.
- **Mitigation Strategies:** To combat these threats, organizations can:
  - Implement strong security protocols and monitoring systems to detect unusual behavior.
  - Use firewalls and intrusion detection systems to limit agent mobility.
  - Regularly update software to patch vulnerabilities that agents may exploit.

6.5.5. Autonomous Mobile Protective Agents

Autonomous mobile protective agents (AMPAs) are advanced software entities designed to enhance cybersecurity by providing real-time protection against various threats. These agents operate independently, leveraging artificial intelligence and machine learning to monitor, detect, and respond to potential security incidents without human intervention.

- Key Features:

i. **Autonomy:** AMPAs function independently, allowing them to continuously assess network environments and adapt to new threats. Their autonomous nature enables them to make decisions based on predefined security protocols and real-time data analysis.

ii. **Mobility:** These agents can navigate across different systems and networks, enabling them to monitor multiple environments simultaneously. This mobility allows AMPAs to provide protection wherever needed, regardless of location.

iii. **Proactive Defense:** Unlike traditional security measures that often react to threats after they occur, AMPAs can predict and prevent potential attacks. By analyzing patterns and anomalies in network traffic and user behavior, they can identify vulnerabilities before they are exploited.

- Functions:

i. **Threat Detection**: AMPAs continuously scan for signs of malicious activity, such as unauthorized access attempts or unusual data transfers. Their sophisticated algorithms enable them to recognize even subtle indicators of threats.

ii. **Incident Response**: Upon detecting a threat, AMPAs can initiate automated responses, such as isolating affected systems, alerting security personnel, or deploying countermeasures to neutralize the threat swiftly.

iii. **Data Protection**: By monitoring data access and usage, AMPAs help prevent data breaches and ensure compliance with organizational security policies.

The deployment of autonomous mobile protective agents significantly enhances an organization's cybersecurity posture. Their ability to operate in real time, adapt to evolving threats, and respond proactively can lead to faster incident resolution and reduced risk of security breaches. Integrating AMPAs into existing security frameworks can provide comprehensive protection and foster a more resilient digital environment.

6.6. CRYPTOGRAPHY IN NETWORK SECURITY

Cryptography plays a vital role in network security by providing mechanisms for protecting data confidentiality, integrity, authenticity, and non-repudiation. As networks have evolved, so have the techniques used to secure communications and protect sensitive information from unauthorized access and manipulation. Below, we explore the fundamental aspects of cryptography in network security, its key principles, common algorithms, and practical applications.

- Key Principles of Cryptography:

  i. **Confidentiality:** This ensures that sensitive information is accessible only to authorized users. Cryptographic techniques like encryption transform plaintext into ciphertext, making it unreadable to anyone who does not possess the decryption key.

  ii. **Integrity:** This guarantees that the data has not been altered or tampered with during transmission. Hash functions are often used to create a unique fingerprint (hash) of the original data, which can be checked later to verify that the data remains unchanged.

  iii. **Authentication:** This process verifies the identity of users or devices in a network. Cryptographic techniques such as digital signatures and certificates are used to establish trust between parties.

iv. **Non-Repudiation:** This ensures that once a transaction has been performed, the sender cannot deny having sent the message. Digital signatures play a crucial role in providing non-repudiation.

- Common Cryptographic Algorithms:

i. **Symmetric Key Cryptography:** In this method, the same key is used for both encryption and decryption. Common symmetric algorithms include:

a. **AES (Advanced Encryption Standard)**: A widely used encryption standard that offers strong security and efficiency.

b. **DES (Data Encryption Standard)**: An older standard that has largely been replaced by AES due to its vulnerabilities.

ii. **Asymmetric Key Cryptography:** Also known as public key cryptography, this method uses a pair of keys: a public key for encryption and a private key for decryption. Common asymmetric algorithms include:

a. **RSA (Rivest-Shamir-Adleman)**: A widely used algorithm for secure data transmission, especially in establishing secure connections over the internet.

b. **ECC (Elliptic Curve Cryptography)**: Offers similar security levels as RSA but with smaller key sizes, making it more efficient.

iii. **Hash Functions:** These algorithms generate a fixed-size hash value from input data, ensuring data integrity. Common hash functions include:

a. **SHA-256 (Secure Hash Algorithm)**: Produces a 256-bit hash and is commonly used in blockchain technology and digital signatures.

b. **MD5 (Message-Digest Algorithm 5)**: An older hash function that is now considered insecure for many applications due to vulnerabilities.

- Applications of Cryptography in Network Security:

i. **Secure Communications:** Protocols like TLS (Transport Layer Security) use cryptographic techniques to secure data transmitted over networks, such as in HTTPS connections for secure web browsing.

ii. **Virtual Private Networks (VPNs):** VPNs use encryption to secure data transmitted over public networks, creating a private tunnel for sensitive information.

iii. **Email Security:** Standards like PGP (Pretty Good Privacy) and S/MIME (Secure/Multipurpose Internet Mail Extensions) use cryptography to ensure that emails are encrypted and authentic.

iv. **Digital Signatures:** Used in various applications, including software distribution and financial transactions, digital signatures verify the identity of the sender and the integrity of the message.

v. **Blockchain and Cryptocurrency:** Cryptography underpins the security of blockchain technology, enabling secure and transparent transactions without a central authority.

- Challenges and Future Directions: Despite its importance, cryptography faces challenges such as:

i. **Quantum Computing**: The advent of quantum computers poses a threat to current cryptographic algorithms, particularly those based on factoring large numbers (like RSA). Research is ongoing into post-quantum cryptography to develop algorithms resistant to quantum attacks.

ii. **Key Management**: Properly managing cryptographic keys is crucial. Weak key management can lead to unauthorized access, undermining the benefits of cryptography.

iii. **Implementation Vulnerabilities**: Flaws in the implementation of cryptographic algorithms can introduce vulnerabilities. Regular security audits and updates are essential.

Cryptography is a cornerstone of network security, providing essential protections for data in transit and at rest. As technology continues to evolve, so too will the methods and practices surrounding cryptography. Understanding its principles, algorithms, and applications is vital for safeguarding sensitive information and maintaining trust in digital communications. With ongoing advancements and emerging threats, the field of cryptography will remain critical in the fight against cyber threats.

6.6.1. Network Encryption

Network encryption is a crucial aspect of cybersecurity that involves securing data transmitted across networks by converting it into an unreadable format.

This process protects sensitive information from unauthorized access, ensuring confidentiality and integrity during transmission.

- Key Concepts:
  i. **Encryption Algorithms:** Network encryption employs various algorithms to transform plaintext into ciphertext. Common symmetric algorithms, like AES (Advanced Encryption Standard), use the same key for both encryption and decryption, making them fast and efficient for real-time applications. Asymmetric algorithms, such as RSA (Rivest-Shamir-Adleman), utilize a pair of keys—a public key for encryption and a private key for decryption—providing a secure method for key exchange.
  ii. **Protocols:** Encryption is implemented through various protocols to secure communications. For instance, TLS (transport layer security) is widely used to secure web traffic (HTTPS), ensuring that data exchanged between users and websites remains confidential. VPNs (virtual private networks) also utilize encryption to create secure tunnels over public networks, protecting data from eavesdropping.
- Benefits:
  i. **Data Confidentiality**: By encrypting data, organizations protect sensitive information from interception by malicious actors, ensuring that only authorized parties can access it.
  ii. **Integrity and Authentication**: Encryption helps verify that data has not been altered during transmission and confirms the identity of the parties involved in the communication.
- Challenges: While network encryption is essential, it is not without challenges. Key management is critical; if encryption keys are lost or compromised, the security of the entire system can be jeopardized. Additionally, the computational overhead of encryption can impact performance, especially in high-volume environments.

6.6.2. Browser Encryption

Browser encryption is a critical aspect of online security that protects the data exchanged between a user's web browser and a web server. It ensures that sensitive information, such as passwords, credit card details, and personal data, remains confidential and secure from potential eavesdroppers.

- Key Concepts:

i. **HTTPS:** The most common form of browser encryption is HTTPS (Hypertext Transfer Protocol Secure). HTTPS uses TLS (transport layer security) to encrypt the data transmitted over the internet. When a user accesses a website with HTTPS, a secure connection is established, encrypting the data before it leaves the user's browser. This prevents unauthorized parties from intercepting and reading the data during transmission.

ii. **Encryption Process:** The encryption process involves a handshake between the browser and the server. During this handshake, they exchange cryptographic keys, which are then used to encrypt and decrypt the information being transmitted. This ensures that even if the data is intercepted, it remains unreadable without the correct decryption key.

- Benefits:

i. **Data Security**: Browser encryption protects sensitive information from being accessed by malicious actors. This is especially important when conducting online transactions or entering personal information.

ii. **User Trust**: Websites that utilize HTTPS display a padlock icon in the browser's address bar, signaling to users that their connection is secure. This fosters trust and encourages users to engage with the site.

- Challenges: Despite its benefits, browser encryption is not foolproof. Users must ensure they are visiting legitimate websites, as attackers can create fake sites that also use HTTPS. Additionally, outdated encryption protocols can pose vulnerabilities, making regular updates and security measures essential.

6.6.3. Onion Routing

Onion routing is a technique used to enhance privacy and anonymity in online communications. It achieves this by encrypting and routing data through a series of nodes, or routers, creating a layered encryption process reminiscent of the layers of an onion. This method obscures the sender's identity and the content of the communication, making it difficult for third parties to track users' activities or access their data.

- How It Works:

i. **Layered Encryption:** When a user sends data over the internet using onion routing, the data is encrypted multiple times before it is transmitted. Each layer of encryption corresponds to a node in the routing path. For example, if the data is sent through three nodes, it will be encrypted three times, with each node able to decrypt only its layer.

ii. **Routing Through Nodes:** The encrypted data is sent through a randomly selected path of nodes (also called relays). Each node receives the encrypted data, removes its layer of encryption, and forwards the remaining data to the next node. This process continues until the data reaches its final destination. The final node, known as the exit node, decrypts the last layer and sends the original data to the intended recipient.

iii. **Anonymity:** The sender's IP address is concealed throughout this process, as only the exit node knows the final destination of the data. Each node only knows the previous and the next node in the path, which enhances anonymity.

- Benefits:

i. **Privacy Protection**: Onion routing protects users from surveillance and data collection by obscuring their online activities.

ii. **Censorship Resistance**: It enables users in restrictive environments to bypass censorship and access blocked content.

- Challenges: While onion routing provides significant anonymity benefits, it is not foolproof. Exit nodes can potentially be monitored, exposing the data being transmitted if it is not encrypted end-to-end. Additionally, onion routing can introduce latency due to the multiple layers and routing hops.

6.6.4. IP Security Protocol Suite (IPsec)

IP Security Protocol Suite (IPsec) is a comprehensive set of protocols designed to secure Internet Protocol (IP) communications through encryption and authentication. It operates at the network layer, providing end-to-end security for data packets as they travel across a network, making it a fundamental technology for establishing Virtual Private Networks (VPNs) and securing communications over untrusted networks.

- Key Components:

i. **Protocols:** IPsec comprises two main protocols:

a. **Authentication Header (AH)**: Provides authentication and integrity for IP packets but does not encrypt the data. AH ensures that the sender is verified and that the data has not been altered in transit.

b. **Encapsulating Security Payload (ESP)**: Offers confidentiality, authentication, and integrity by encrypting the data payload. ESP is more commonly used than AH because it provides encryption alongside authentication.

ii. **Security Associations (SAs):** IPsec relies on SAs, which are agreements between devices on how to secure communications. Each SA defines the protocols and keys used for encryption and authentication, ensuring both parties have a mutual understanding of security measures.

- Modes of Operation: IPsec can operate in two primary modes:

i. **Transport Mode**: Only the payload of the IP packet is encrypted and/or authenticated. The original IP header remains intact, making this mode suitable for end-to-end communication between hosts.

ii. **Tunnel Mode**: The entire IP packet, including the header, is encapsulated within a new IP packet with a new header. This mode is typically used for VPNs, providing security for traffic traveling across untrusted networks by creating a secure tunnel.

- Benefits:

i. **Enhanced Security**: IPsec provides robust security features that protect data from eavesdropping, tampering, and forgery.

ii. **Interoperability**: As a standardized protocol suite, IPsec works across various platforms and devices, enabling secure communications between different systems.

- Challenges: Despite its advantages, implementing IPsec can be complex due to configuration requirements and the potential for performance overhead. Moreover, managing keys and security associations can introduce additional challenges.

6.6.5. Virtual Private Networks

A Virtual Private Network (VPN) is a technology that creates a secure and encrypted connection over a less secure network, such as the Internet. VPNs enable users to send and receive data as if their devices were directly connected to a private network, enhancing privacy and security by masking IP addresses and encrypting data.

- Benefits of VPNs:
  - i. **Enhanced Security:** VPNs encrypt data, making it difficult for unauthorized users to intercept and read information, which is particularly important for sensitive transactions and communications.
  - ii. **Anonymity:** By masking a user's IP address, VPNs help protect privacy, making it harder for websites and advertisers to track online activities.
  - iii. **Access to Restricted Content:** VPNs allow users to bypass geographic restrictions and access content that may be blocked in their region, such as streaming services or specific websites.
- Types of VPNs:
  - i. **Remote Access VPN:** This type enables individual users to connect to a private network from a remote location. Remote access VPNs are commonly used by employees working from home or traveling. They provide secure access to company resources, applications, and data.
  - ii. **Site-to-Site VPN:** This type connects entire networks to each other, allowing secure communication between multiple sites, such as branch offices and headquarters. Site-to-site VPNs are commonly used in businesses to facilitate secure interoffice communications.
  - iii. **Client-to-Site VPN:** A subset of remote access VPNs, this type allows individual devices to connect to a corporate network. Users install VPN client software on their devices to establish a secure connection to the network.
  - iv. **MPLS VPN (Multiprotocol Label Switching):** This is a service offered by internet service providers (ISPs) to create a private network across a wide area. It uses labels to route packets more efficiently, making it suitable for businesses that require reliable and secure communications.
  - v. **SSL/TLS VPN:** These VPNs use Secure Socket Layer (SSL) or Transport Layer Security (TLS) protocols to secure data. They are often easier to configure and use, making them ideal for accessing web applications securely (Figure 6.12).

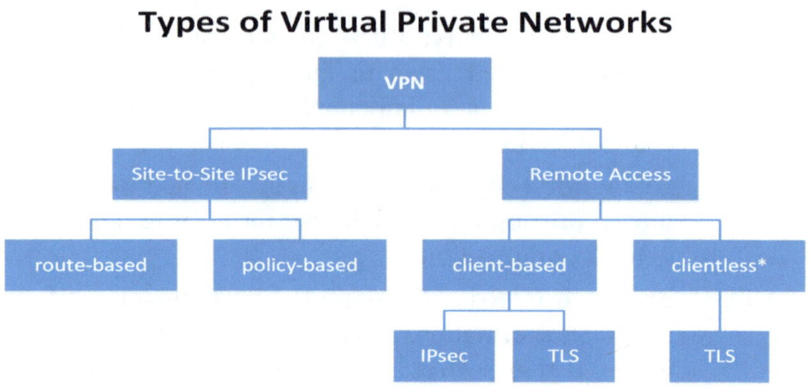

Figure 6.12. Types of VPNs.

6.6.6. System Architecture

System architecture refers to the conceptual model that defines the structure, behavior, and more views of a system. It serves as a blueprint for both the system and its components, detailing how they interact and operate within a broader context. This discipline is essential in fields like software engineering, information technology, and network design.

- Key Components:

  i. **Architecture Patterns:** Various patterns exist to guide system design. Common patterns include:

  a. **Layered Architecture**: Divides the system into layers, such as presentation, business logic, and data access, promoting separation of concerns and easier maintenance.

  b. **Microservices Architecture**: Breaks applications into small, independently deployable services, allowing for scalability and flexibility.

  c. **Client-Server Architecture**: Involves clients requesting services from centralized servers, commonly used in web applications.

  ii. **Components:** System architecture encompasses various components, including hardware, software, networks, and databases. Each component plays a specific role in achieving the system's functionality and performance.

  iii. **Interfaces:** Interfaces define how components communicate with each other. Well-designed interfaces facilitate interaction between different parts of the system and external systems, ensuring smooth data flow and functionality.

- Design Considerations: When designing a system architecture, several factors must be considered:
  i. **Scalability**: The ability of the system to grow and handle increased loads efficiently.
  ii. **Performance**: Ensuring that the system meets responsiveness and speed requirements.
  iii. **Security**: Implementing measures to protect the system from threats and vulnerabilities.
  iv. **Maintainability**: Designing for ease of updates and changes, allowing for long-term sustainability.
- Importance: Effective system architecture is critical for successful project outcomes. It provides a framework for making design decisions and helps stakeholders understand how the system will meet business requirements. A well-defined architecture minimizes risks, improves resource allocation, and enhances collaboration among teams.

6.7. FIREWALLS

Firewalls are essential security devices or software applications that monitor and control incoming and outgoing network traffic based on predetermined security rules. They serve as a barrier between trusted internal networks and untrusted external networks, such as the Internet, helping to protect systems from unauthorized access and cyber threats.

- Types of Firewalls:
  i. **Packet-Filtering Firewalls:** These are the most basic type of firewalls. They analyze packets of data and allow or block them based on user-defined rules such as IP addresses, protocols, and port numbers. While effective for simple filtering, they do not inspect the content of the packets, which can leave systems vulnerable.
  ii. **Stateful Inspection Firewalls:** These firewalls maintain records of active connections and make filtering decisions based on the state of the connection. They track the state of network connections and can provide more advanced filtering compared to packet-filtering firewalls, offering better security without sacrificing performance.

iii. **Application Layer Firewalls:** Also known as proxy firewalls, these operate at the application layer and inspect the data packets in detail. They can filter traffic based on specific applications or services, providing granular control over web traffic, email, and other application protocols. This type of firewall is more resource-intensive but offers superior security.

iv. **Next-Generation Firewalls (NGFW):** These incorporate advanced features such as intrusion prevention systems (IPS), deep packet inspection (DPI), and application awareness. NGFWs are designed to detect and block sophisticated attacks while providing more comprehensive monitoring and control (Figure 6.13).

Figure 6.13. Different types of firewalls.

- Benefits:

i. **Enhanced Security**: Firewalls help prevent unauthorized access to networks and systems, acting as a first line of defense against cyber threats.

ii. **Traffic Monitoring**: They provide insights into network traffic, helping identify suspicious activity and potential security breaches.

iii. **Access Control**: Firewalls enable organizations to enforce policies regarding which users or devices can access specific resources.

- Challenges: Despite their importance, firewalls are not foolproof. They require regular updates and management to adapt to evolving threats. Additionally, misconfigured firewalls can lead to security gaps, so ongoing monitoring and adjustment are crucial.

6.7.1. What Is a Firewall?

A firewall is a network security device or software application designed to monitor and control incoming and outgoing network traffic based on predetermined security rules. It acts as a protective barrier between trusted internal networks and untrusted external networks, such as the Internet, helping to safeguard sensitive data and systems from unauthorized access, cyber threats, and malicious activities.

- How Firewalls Work: Firewalls inspect data packets transmitted across the network. They analyze various attributes of these packets, including source and destination IP addresses, protocols, and port numbers, to determine whether to allow or block traffic. By implementing specific security rules, firewalls can effectively filter unwanted traffic and protect the integrity of the network.
- Importance of Firewalls: Firewalls are crucial for maintaining network security. They help prevent unauthorized access, mitigate the risk of data breaches, and enforce security policies within an organization. By implementing effective firewall solutions, businesses can significantly enhance their overall security posture and protect critical assets from potential cyber threats.

6.7.2. Design of Firewalls

The design of firewalls is a critical aspect of network security, aimed at creating a robust barrier between trusted internal networks and untrusted external networks. Effective firewall design involves several key considerations, including architecture, functionality, and management.

1. Architecture: Firewalls can be deployed in various configurations:
   - **i.** **Network-based Firewalls**: These are hardware devices placed at the network perimeter, monitoring traffic between internal and external networks. They protect multiple devices and systems simultaneously, offering centralized control.
   - **ii.** **Host-based Firewalls**: Installed on individual devices, these firewalls protect specific endpoints. They are particularly useful for securing laptops and mobile devices that may connect to different networks.
   - **iii.** **Cloud Firewalls**: As more organizations adopt cloud services, cloud-based firewalls offer scalability and flexibility, protecting cloud environments and applications.

2. Functionality: A well-designed firewall should incorporate several functionalities:
   i. **Packet Filtering**: Inspecting packets based on predetermined rules to allow or block traffic based on IP addresses, protocols, and port numbers.
   ii. **Stateful Inspection**: Maintaining records of active connections to determine the legitimacy of incoming packets, providing enhanced security.
   iii. **Deep Packet Inspection (DPI)**: Analyzing the content of packets beyond header information, allowing for the detection of malicious payloads or applications.
   iv. **Intrusion Prevention Systems (IPS)**: Integrated systems that monitor traffic for signs of malicious activity, automatically blocking or alerting administrators to potential threats.
3. Management and Policy Configuration: Effective firewall management is crucial for maintaining security. This involves:
   i. **Rule Configuration**: Defining and regularly updating access control lists (ACLs) that specify which traffic is allowed or denied. The principle of least privilege should guide these rules.
   ii. **Logging and Monitoring**: Implementing logging mechanisms to track traffic patterns and potential threats, facilitating timely responses to security incidents.
   iii. **Regular Updates**: Keeping firewall firmware and software up to date to protect against emerging vulnerabilities.

6.7.3. Personal Firewalls

Personal firewalls are software applications designed to protect individual computers and devices from unauthorized access and cyber threats. Unlike network firewalls, which secure entire networks, personal firewalls focus on safeguarding the host system, making them essential for home users and remote workers.

- Key Features:
  i. **Traffic Monitoring:** Personal firewalls continuously monitor incoming and outgoing traffic, analyzing data packets for suspicious activity. They can block unauthorized connections while allowing legitimate traffic, thus preventing malware and hackers from accessing the system.

ii. **Application Control:** Many personal firewalls include application control features that allow users to define which applications can access the Internet. This ensures that only trusted programs can communicate online, reducing the risk of malware propagation.

iii. **Intrusion Detection and Prevention:** Personal firewalls often incorporate intrusion detection systems (IDS) to identify and alert users about potential threats or suspicious activities, enabling proactive responses to security incidents.

iv. **Customizable Rules:** Users can create and modify rules for traffic management, specifying which ports and protocols are allowed or blocked. This customization enhances security by tailoring protections to individual needs.

- Benefits:

i. **Enhanced Security**: Personal firewalls provide an additional layer of security, particularly for devices that connect to public or unsecured networks, such as Wi-Fi hotspots.

ii. **User-Friendly Interfaces**: Most personal firewalls are designed for ease of use, featuring graphical user interfaces (GUIs) that allow users to configure settings without advanced technical knowledge.

Ø Challenges: While personal firewalls are beneficial, they can sometimes generate false positives, blocking legitimate traffic or applications. Additionally, they require regular updates to stay effective against new threats.

6.7.4. Comparison of Firewall Types

When choosing a firewall for network security, it's essential to understand the differences between various types. Each firewall type has unique features, strengths, and weaknesses, making them suitable for different environments and security needs. Here's a comparison of the main types of firewalls:

1. Packet-Filtering Firewalls:

i. **Functionality**: Operate at the network layer, inspecting packets based on IP addresses, protocols, and port numbers.

ii. **Pros**: Fast and efficient; low resource consumption.

iii. **Cons**: Limited security as they do not inspect the content of packets, making them vulnerable to certain attacks.

2. Stateful Inspection Firewalls:
    i. **Functionality**: Track active connections and maintain a state table, allowing only packets that match established connections.
    ii. **Pros**: Enhanced security compared to packet-filtering firewalls; capable of understanding the context of traffic.
    iii. **Cons**: More resource-intensive than basic packet filters; may introduce latency.
3. Application Layer Firewalls (Proxy Firewalls):
    i. **Functionality**: Operate at the application layer, inspecting the content of data packets and filtering based on application-specific rules.
    ii. **Pros**: Provide granular control over traffic and protect against application-layer attacks (e.g., SQL injection).
    iii. **Cons**: Slower due to deep packet inspection; can be more complex to configure.
4. Next-Generation Firewalls (NGFW):
    i. **Functionality**: Combine traditional firewall features with advanced capabilities like intrusion prevention, application awareness, and deep packet inspection.
    ii. **Pros**: Comprehensive protection against sophisticated attacks; capable of monitoring and controlling application traffic.
    iii. **Cons**: Higher cost and complexity; require more resources to operate effectively.
5. Web Application Firewalls (WAF):
    i. **Functionality**: Specifically designed to protect web applications by filtering and monitoring HTTP traffic.
    ii. **Pros**: Effective against common web vulnerabilities and attacks like XSS and SQL injection; can be customized for specific applications.
    iii. **Cons**: Limited to web application traffic; may not provide complete network security.

6.7.5. Example Firewall Configurations

Firewall configurations are essential for defining security policies that control network traffic. Here are a few examples of common firewall configurations:

1. Basic Packet Filtering Configuration: In a simple home network, a packet-filtering firewall might be set up to allow only specific types of traffic. For example:
   - **i. Allow**: HTTP (port 80) and HTTPS (port 443) traffic to allow web browsing.
   - **ii. Deny**: All incoming traffic by default, blocking unsolicited requests from external sources.
   - **iii. Allow**: Outgoing traffic on specific ports (e.g., SMTP on port 25) for sending emails.
2. Stateful Inspection Configuration: For a small business, a stateful inspection firewall could be configured to maintain the state of connections:
   - **i. Allow**: Established connections to continue (e.g., a user accessing a web server).
   - **ii. Deny**: Any new incoming connections that are not part of an established session.
   - **iii. Log**: All denied attempts to identify potential threats or unauthorized access attempts.
3. Application Layer Firewall Configuration: In a corporate environment, an application layer firewall might be configured as follows:
   - **i. Allow**: Traffic from a specific IP range (e.g., internal users) to access corporate applications on specific ports (e.g., 8080 for a web application).
   - **ii. Deny**: All access to the application from external IP addresses unless explicitly allowed (e.g., a VPN).
   - **iii. Inspect**: Incoming requests for SQL injection patterns and block suspicious traffic.
4. Next-Generation Firewall Configuration: For a large enterprise, an NGFW could include advanced configurations:
   - **i. Allow**: Legitimate traffic for specific applications (e.g., Salesforce, Office 365) while blocking known malicious IP addresses using threat intelligence feeds.
   - **ii. Enable**: Intrusion prevention features to block specific attack patterns.
   - **iii. Implement**: User identity-based rules to apply different policies based on user roles.

6.7.6. Network Address Translation (NAT)

Network address translation (NAT) is a technique used in networking that enables the mapping of private, internal IP addresses to a public IP address and vice versa. This process helps manage IP address space, enhances security, and facilitates the connection of multiple devices to the Internet using a single public IP address.

- Key Functions of NAT:
  - i. **IP Address Conservation:** NAT allows multiple devices on a local network to share a single public IP address. This is particularly useful in environments where IP addresses are limited, such as in homes and small businesses.
  - ii. **Security Enhancement:** By hiding internal IP addresses, NAT adds a layer of security. External users cannot directly access devices within the private network, making it harder for attackers to exploit vulnerabilities.
  - iii. **Traffic Management:** NAT can also help manage traffic by directing incoming requests to the appropriate internal device. For example, if a request comes in for a specific port, NAT can route it to the designated internal device based on preconfigured rules.
- Types of NAT:
  - i. **Static NAT:** Maps a single public IP address to a single private IP address. This is useful for services that need to be consistently accessible from outside the network, such as web servers.
  - ii. **Dynamic NAT:** Uses a pool of public IP addresses and assigns them to internal devices as needed. This method is less predictable than static NAT but still allows multiple devices to connect.
  - iii. **Port Address Translation (PAT):** Also known as "NAT overload," this type allows multiple devices to be mapped to a single public IP address by differentiating connections based on port numbers. It is the most common form of NAT used in home routers.

6.7.7. Data Loss Prevention

Data Loss Prevention (DLP) refers to a set of strategies and technologies designed to ensure that sensitive data is not lost, misused, or accessed by unauthorized individuals. DLP is critical for organizations that handle confidential information, such as personally identifiable information (PII), financial records, and intellectual property.

- Key Components of DLP:
  i. **Data Identification:** The first step in any DLP strategy is identifying sensitive data within an organization. This can involve scanning files, databases, and communications to classify data based on its sensitivity and importance.
  ii. **Data Monitoring:** DLP solutions continuously monitor data in use, in transit, and at rest. This involves tracking user activities, data transfers, and communications to detect potential risks or breaches. For instance, monitoring email attachments or file transfers can help identify unauthorized sharing of sensitive information.
  iii. **Policy Enforcement:** Organizations define policies that dictate how sensitive data should be handled. DLP solutions enforce these policies by blocking, alerting, or encrypting data transfers that violate established rules. For example, if an employee attempts to send a confidential document via email, the DLP system can block the action and notify the user.
  iv. **Incident Response:** DLP tools provide reporting and analytics capabilities to help organizations respond to data breaches or policy violations. This includes alerting security teams, providing detailed logs, and facilitating forensic investigations.
- Benefits of DLP:
  i. **Compliance**: DLP helps organizations comply with regulations such as GDPR, HIPAA, and PCI DSS by protecting sensitive data and avoiding costly fines.
  ii. **Risk Mitigation**: By preventing unauthorized access and data leaks, DLP reduces the risk of data breaches and the associated financial and reputational damage.

6.7.8. Intrusion Detection and Prevention Systems

Intrusion Detection and Prevention Systems (IDPS) are critical components of network security designed to identify and respond to potential security threats and attacks. These systems monitor network traffic, analyze behavior, and provide alerts or take action to prevent unauthorized access to sensitive information and resources. The growing complexity of cyber threats necessitates the use of IDPS to safeguard organizations' networks and data.

- Key Functions of IDPS:

i. **Monitoring and Analysis:** IDPS continuously monitors network traffic for suspicious activities and patterns that may indicate a security breach. This involves analyzing data packets, user behavior, and system logs to detect anomalies.

ii. **Detection Methods:** IDPS utilize various detection methods:

a. **Signature-based Detection**: This method relies on known patterns of malicious activity, such as specific malware signatures. Signature-based systems are effective against known threats but may fail to detect new, unknown attacks.

b. **Anomaly-based Detection**: This approach establishes a baseline of normal network behavior and flags deviations from this baseline. It is useful for detecting zero-day attacks and other novel threats but may generate false positives if the baseline is not accurately defined.

c. **Behavioral Detection**: Behavioral analysis examines user and system behavior to identify unusual patterns. For example, if a user suddenly accesses sensitive files they typically do not use, the system can flag this as a potential threat.

iii. **Alerting:** When an intrusion or suspicious activity is detected, IDPS generate alerts to notify security personnel. Alerts can range from simple notifications to detailed reports that include information about the nature of the threat and suggested remediation steps.

iv. **Prevention:** In addition to detecting threats, many IDPS can take proactive measures to prevent attacks. This can include:

a. **Blocking Traffic**: Automatically blocking malicious traffic or unauthorized access attempts based on predefined rules.

b. **Isolation**: Isolating affected systems from the network to contain potential breaches.

c. **Session Termination**: Ending active sessions that exhibit suspicious behavior.

- Types of IDPS:

i. **Network-based Intrusion Detection and Prevention Systems (NIDPS):** NIDPS are deployed at critical points within the network, such as gateways or network segments, to monitor traffic entering and exiting the network. They analyze packet data and provide real-time detection and prevention of threats across the entire network.

ii. **Host-based Intrusion Detection and Prevention Systems (HIDPS):** HIDPS are installed on individual devices or servers, monitoring system-level activities such as file access, user logins, and application behavior. This type of system is effective for detecting attacks that may bypass network defenses, such as malware infections.

iii. **Wireless Intrusion Detection and Prevention Systems (WIDPS):** WIDPS are specifically designed to monitor wireless networks for unauthorized access attempts, rogue access points, and other wireless threats. They provide insights into wireless network security and help organizations protect against vulnerabilities unique to wireless environments.

iv. **Hybrid Systems:** Some solutions combine the features of both network-based and host-based systems, offering a comprehensive approach to intrusion detection and prevention.

- **Strategies:** Implementing IDPS involves several strategic considerations:

i. **Environment Assessment:** Understanding the network architecture, data flow, and critical assets is essential for determining the optimal placement of IDPS. Organizations should assess where sensitive data resides and identify potential attack vectors.

ii. **Configuration:** Properly configuring IDPS is crucial to minimize false positives and ensure effective detection. This includes defining rules, policies, and thresholds tailored to the organization's specific security needs.

iii. **Integration with Other Security Tools:** IDPS should be integrated with other security solutions, such as firewalls, Security Information and Event Management (SIEM) systems, and endpoint protection tools. This creates a multi-layered security approach, enhancing overall threat detection and response capabilities.

iv. **Regular Updates and Maintenance:** To remain effective, IDPS must be regularly updated with the latest signatures, threat intelligence, and software patches. Continuous monitoring and periodic assessments ensure the system adapts to evolving threats.

- **Challenges:** While IDPS offer significant benefits, they also face challenges:
  - **i. False Positives:** One of the primary challenges is managing false positives, which can overwhelm security teams and divert attention from genuine threats. Tuning the system to reduce false alerts without compromising detection capability is essential.
  - **ii. Resource Intensive:** Continuous monitoring and analysis can require substantial system resources, especially in high-traffic networks. Organizations must balance the need for comprehensive monitoring with the potential impact on network performance.
  - **iii. Evolving Threat Landscape:** Cyber threats are constantly evolving, with attackers developing new techniques to bypass traditional defenses. IDPS must adapt to these changes to remain effective, requiring ongoing investment in updates and improvements.

Intrusion detection and prevention systems are vital for safeguarding networks against a myriad of cyber threats. By monitoring, analyzing, and responding to suspicious activities, IDPS provide organizations with enhanced security capabilities. However, to maximize effectiveness, organizations must carefully consider deployment strategies, integration with existing security tools, and ongoing maintenance. As the cybersecurity landscape continues to evolve, the role of IDPS will remain crucial in defending against increasingly sophisticated attacks.

6.7.9. Types of IDSs

Intrusion Detection Systems (IDS) are critical for monitoring and analyzing network traffic to identify suspicious activities and potential security breaches. They come in various types; each suited to different environments and security needs. Here are the main types of IDS:

1. Network-based Intrusion Detection Systems (NIDS): NIDS monitor network traffic across multiple devices and analyze the data packets flowing through the network. They are typically deployed at key points, such as network gateways or segments, to provide a broad view of all traffic. NIDS can detect a variety of attacks, including denial-of-service (DoS) attacks and port scanning, making them essential for overall network security.

2. Host-based Intrusion Detection Systems (HIDS): These are installed on individual devices or servers to monitor system-level activities. They analyze logs, file integrity, and user actions to detect unauthorized access or malicious behavior on that specific host. HIDS are particularly effective at identifying insider threats and can provide detailed insights into events occurring on the device itself.
3. Hybrid Intrusion Detection Systems: These combine the features of both NIDS and HIDS, allowing organizations to benefit from comprehensive monitoring across both network and host levels. This dual approach enhances detection capabilities, as it can identify threats that may bypass one type of system. Hybrid systems are particularly effective in complex environments where multiple attack vectors exist.
4. Wireless Intrusion Detection Systems (WIDS): These are specialized for monitoring wireless networks, detecting unauthorized access points, rogue devices, and wireless-specific attacks. They help secure Wi-Fi environments, which are often more vulnerable to attacks due to their broadcast nature.

6.7.10. Other Intrusion Detection Technology

While traditional Intrusion Detection Systems (IDS) play a crucial role in network security, several other technologies and approaches can enhance threat detection and response capabilities. These technologies work either independently or in conjunction with IDS to provide a more comprehensive security posture. Below are some notable alternatives and complementary technologies:

1. **Intrusion Prevention Systems (IPS):** This extends the capabilities of traditional IDS by not only detecting threats but also taking proactive measures to prevent them. IPS can automatically block or reject malicious traffic based on predefined rules and policies. This capability allows organizations to respond to threats in real-time, minimizing the potential damage.

   IPS can be deployed inline (in the path of the network traffic) or out-of-band (monitoring traffic without altering its flow). Inline deployment allows immediate action against detected threats, while out-of-band systems can alert administrators without interfering with network operations.
2. **Security Information and Event Management (SIEM):** These systems aggregate and analyze security data from multiple sources,

including firewalls, servers, and endpoint devices. By collecting logs and event data in real-time, SIEM provides a centralized view of the security landscape.

The benefits of SIEM include:

i. **Correlation and Analysis:** SIEM tools can correlate events from different sources to identify complex attack patterns that might be missed by standalone systems.

ii. **Incident Response:** Automated alerts and incident response workflows help security teams respond more effectively to potential threats.

iii. **Compliance Reporting:** SIEM systems often include features for generating compliance reports, making it easier to adhere to regulations.

3. **Endpoint Detection and Response (EDR):** These solutions focus on monitoring and securing endpoints—such as laptops, desktops, and servers—against potential threats. EDR tools collect detailed telemetry data from endpoints, enabling the detection of suspicious activities and providing insights into potential breaches.

Key features of EDR include:

i. **Real-Time Monitoring**: Continuous monitoring of endpoint activities allows for the quick identification of anomalous behavior.

ii. **Threat Hunting**: Security analysts can proactively search for threats within the endpoint data, improving the organization's overall security posture.

iii. **Forensics and Response**: EDR tools provide forensic capabilities to investigate incidents, enabling organizations to understand the attack vector and improve defenses.

4. **Behavioral Analytics:** Behavioral analytics leverage machine learning and artificial intelligence to establish baselines of normal behavior for users and systems. By analyzing patterns and deviations from established norms, these systems can detect potential security incidents that traditional methods might overlook.

Benefits of behavioral analytics include:

i. **Early Threat Detection**: Identifying unusual patterns can lead to early detection of insider threats, account takeovers, or advanced persistent threats (APTs).

ii. **Reduced False Positives**: By focusing on behavior rather than specific signatures, these systems can reduce the number of false alarms, allowing security teams to focus on genuine threats.

5. **Network Traffic Analysis (NTA):** These tools monitor network traffic flows to identify suspicious patterns and anomalies. NTA solutions can detect various types of attacks, including data exfiltration and lateral movement within the network.

Key features of NTA include:

i. **Flow Analysis**: By examining network flows rather than individual packets, NTA can provide insights into traffic patterns and potential threats.

ii. **Anomaly Detection**: Machine learning algorithms can be employed to identify unusual traffic behavior, which may indicate a breach or attempted attack.

iii. **Integration with Other Tools**: NTA can complement existing security measures by providing additional context for alerts generated by IDS or SIEM systems.

6. **Threat Intelligence Platforms:** Threat intelligence platforms collect, analyze, and disseminate information about emerging threats and vulnerabilities. By integrating threat intelligence into security operations, organizations can enhance their incident detection and response capabilities.

Benefits of threat intelligence include:

i. **Proactive Defense**: Knowing about potential threats in advance allows organizations to strengthen their defenses before an attack occurs.

ii. **Contextual Awareness**: Threat intelligence provides context for alerts generated by IDS and other security tools, helping analysts prioritize responses based on threat severity and relevance.

7. **Deception Technology:** This involves creating decoy assets (such as fake servers or databases) to lure attackers away from real assets. When attackers interact with these decoys, security teams can detect and respond to their actions in real-time.

Advantages of deception technology include:

i. **Early Detection**: Decoys can reveal attacker methodologies and techniques, allowing for quicker responses.

ii. **Threat Intelligence Generation**: Interactions with decoys can provide valuable data on attacker behavior and tactics.

The evolving threat landscape necessitates a multi-layered security approach that goes beyond traditional Intrusion Detection Systems. By incorporating additional technologies such as Intrusion Prevention Systems, SIEM, EDR, behavioral analytics, and more, organizations can enhance their ability to detect, respond to, and mitigate cyber threats. Combining these solutions creates a robust security posture that not only protects critical assets but also empowers security teams with actionable intelligence to stay ahead of potential attacks. As cyber threats become increasingly sophisticated, adopting a diverse set of security technologies is essential for safeguarding organizational data and infrastructure.

6.7.11. Intrusion Prevention Systems

Intrusion Prevention Systems (IPS) are essential components of modern cybersecurity strategies, designed to detect and respond to potential threats in real-time. Unlike traditional Intrusion Detection Systems (IDS), which primarily focus on identifying suspicious activity, IPS actively take measures to prevent intrusions, making them a proactive defense mechanism.

- Key Functions of IPS:

i. **Traffic Monitoring and Analysis:** IPS continuously monitors network traffic for signs of malicious activity. It analyzes data packets as they traverse the network, inspecting headers and payloads to identify potentially harmful patterns or signatures.

ii. **Threat Detection:** IPS employs various detection techniques, including:

a. **Signature-based Detection**: This method relies on predefined patterns of known threats. The system compares incoming traffic against a database of known attack signatures. While effective against recognized threats, this approach may struggle with new or unknown attacks.

b. **Anomaly-based Detection**: IPS establishes a baseline of normal network behavior and identifies deviations from this norm. By flagging unusual patterns, this method can detect zero-day vulnerabilities and novel attacks that lack known signatures.

c. **Behavioral Detection**: Similar to anomaly detection, this method analyzes the behavior of users and systems. It flags actions that are inconsistent with established user profiles or historical activity, aiding in the identification of insider threats and compromised accounts.

iii. **Automated Response:** Upon detecting a potential threat, an IPS can automatically take action to prevent it. This may include:

a. **Blocking Traffic**: The IPS can drop malicious packets or terminate suspicious connections based on predefined rules.

b. **Session Termination**: Active sessions that exhibit abnormal behavior can be terminated to prevent further unauthorized access.

c. **Alerts and Notifications**: The system can generate alerts to notify security personnel of potential incidents, providing detailed information for further investigation.

iv. **Logging and Reporting:** IPS solutions maintain logs of detected threats and actions taken. This data is vital for compliance reporting, forensic analysis, and refining security policies.

- Types of IPS:

i. **Network-based Intrusion Prevention Systems (NIPS):** NIPS are deployed at key points in a network, such as gateways or network segments, to monitor all incoming and outgoing traffic. They analyze data flows in real time, providing protection against network-based attacks, such as denial-of-service (DoS) and network scans.

ii. **Host-based Intrusion Prevention Systems (HIPS):** HIPS are installed on individual devices (like servers and endpoints) to monitor system-level activities. They provide insights into file integrity, application behavior, and user actions, making them effective for detecting insider threats and local exploits.

iii. **Wireless Intrusion Prevention Systems (WIPS):** WIPS specifically focus on monitoring wireless networks. They detect unauthorized access points, rogue devices, and wireless-specific attacks, helping secure Wi-Fi environments that are often more vulnerable to threats.

iv. **Cloud-based Intrusion Prevention Systems:** With the increasing adoption of cloud services, cloud-based IPS solutions monitor traffic to and from cloud environments. These systems are designed to protect cloud applications and data from various threats, offering scalability and flexibility.

- **Benefits of IPS:**

  i. **Proactive Defense:** The primary advantage of IPS is its proactive nature. By actively blocking malicious traffic and preventing unauthorized access, IPS significantly reduces the risk of data breaches and cyberattacks.

  ii. **Real-Time Protection:** IPS operates in real-time, allowing organizations to respond to threats immediately. This capability is crucial for minimizing damage and ensuring the integrity of systems and data.

  iii. **Comprehensive Coverage:** By monitoring network traffic, host activities, and wireless communications, IPS provides a multi-layered approach to security, enhancing the overall protection of the organization's infrastructure.

  iv. **Regulatory Compliance:** Many industries are subject to regulations that mandate robust security measures. Implementing IPS helps organizations meet compliance requirements by demonstrating a commitment to protecting sensitive data.

  v. **Improved Incident Response:** With automated response capabilities, IPS enables security teams to focus on high-priority tasks, streamlining incident response processes and reducing the time required to mitigate threats.

- Challenges and Considerations:

  i. **False Positives:** One of the significant challenges with IPS is the potential for false positives, where legitimate traffic is flagged as malicious. High false positive rates can lead to alert fatigue among security teams, causing them to overlook genuine threats.

  ii. **Resource Intensive:** IPS systems can be resource-intensive, requiring significant processing power and bandwidth to analyze traffic effectively. Organizations must ensure they have the necessary infrastructure to support their IPS deployments.

  iii. **Complex Configuration:** Properly configuring an IPS to balance security and usability can be complex. Organizations must carefully define rules and policies to avoid unnecessary disruptions to legitimate activities.

  iv. **Evolving Threat Landscape:** The constantly evolving nature of cyber threats means that IPS must be regularly updated with new signatures, patterns, and policies to remain effective against emerging attacks.

- **Best Practices for Implementing IPS:**
  i. **Integration with Other Security Tools:** IPS should be integrated with other security solutions, such as firewalls and Security Information and Event Management (SIEM) systems. This creates a cohesive security architecture that enhances threat detection and response.
  ii. **Regular Updates and Maintenance:** Organizations must keep their IPS up to date with the latest signatures and threat intelligence. Regular maintenance ensures optimal performance and effectiveness in detecting new threats.
  iii. **Continuous Monitoring and Tuning:** Ongoing monitoring and tuning of the IPS are crucial for minimizing false positives and ensuring that the system adapts to changes in the network environment.
  iv. **Training and Awareness:** Security teams should be trained on the capabilities and limitations of the IPS. Raising awareness about potential threats and the importance of prompt responses is vital for maintaining a robust security posture.

Intrusion Prevention Systems are vital components of an organization's cybersecurity strategy. By actively monitoring, detecting, and preventing unauthorized access, IPS significantly enhance the security of networks and systems. While they present certain challenges, implementing best practices can help organizations maximize the benefits of IPS, providing a proactive defense against a constantly evolving threat landscape. As cyber threats become more sophisticated, the role of IPS will continue to grow, making them an indispensable element of modern security frameworks.

6.7.12. Intrusion Response

Intrusion response refers to the set of actions taken by an organization when a security breach or intrusion is detected. An effective response is crucial for mitigating damage, preserving evidence, and restoring normal operations. A well-defined intrusion response plan (IRP) enables organizations to react promptly and effectively to incidents.

- **Key Components of Intrusion Response:**
  i. **Preparation:** Before an incident occurs, organizations should establish a comprehensive IRP. This includes defining roles and responsibilities, creating communication plans, and ensuring that staff are trained to recognize and report

suspicious activities. Regularly testing and updating the plan is essential for effectiveness.

ii. **Detection and Analysis:** When an intrusion is detected, the first step is to analyze the situation. Security teams use tools such as Intrusion Detection Systems (IDS), Security Information and Event Management (SIEM) solutions, and log analysis to determine the nature and scope of the attack. Accurate analysis helps in understanding whether it's a false positive or a genuine threat.

iii. **Containment:** Once an intrusion is confirmed, the immediate goal is to contain the incident to prevent further damage. This may involve isolating affected systems, blocking malicious traffic, or disabling compromised accounts. Quick containment is critical to limit the spread of the intrusion.

iv. **Eradication:** After containment, the next step is to identify the root cause of the intrusion and eliminate it. This may involve removing malware, closing vulnerabilities, and applying patches. Ensuring that the threat has been fully eradicated is essential before restoring services.

v. **Recovery:** Once the threat has been addressed, affected systems can be restored to normal operations. This process may involve restoring data from backups and monitoring systems closely for any signs of lingering threats.

vi. **Post-Incident Review:** After resolving the incident, conducting a post-incident review is vital. This includes analyzing the response process, identifying areas for improvement, and updating the IRP to enhance future incident handling.

Effective intrusion response is a critical aspect of an organization's cybersecurity strategy. By preparing, detecting, containing, eradicating, recovering, and reviewing, organizations can minimize the impact of security incidents and strengthen their defenses against future threats.

6.7.13. Goals for Intrusion Detection Systems

Intrusion Detection Systems (IDS) play a pivotal role in cybersecurity by monitoring network traffic and identifying potential threats. The primary goals of IDS are essential for ensuring the security and integrity of information systems. Here are the key objectives:

1. **Threat Detection:** The foremost goal of an IDS is to identify unauthorized access and malicious activities in real time. This includes detecting various types of attacks, such as malware infections, denial-of-service (DoS) attacks, and intrusion attempts. Effective threat detection allows organizations to respond swiftly to mitigate potential damage.
2. **Incident Response Facilitation:** IDS aims to support and enhance incident response efforts. By providing alerts and detailed reports on detected threats, IDS assists security teams in understanding the nature and scope of an intrusion. This information is crucial for making informed decisions about containment and remediation strategies.
3. **Vulnerability Identification:** An effective IDS helps organizations identify vulnerabilities within their systems. By analyzing patterns of suspicious activity, IDS can reveal weaknesses that may be exploited by attackers, allowing organizations to strengthen their defenses proactively.
4. **Compliance and Reporting:** Many industries are subject to regulatory requirements that mandate monitoring and reporting on security incidents. IDS can assist in compliance by providing logs and reports that demonstrate adherence to security standards, such as PCI DSS or HIPAA. This capability is vital for audits and maintaining trust with stakeholders.
5. **Continuous Monitoring:** A core goal of IDS is to provide ongoing surveillance of network traffic and system activities. Continuous monitoring helps organizations stay aware of potential threats and emerging attack vectors, enabling a proactive rather than reactive security posture.
6. **Data Integrity and Confidentiality:** IDS aims to protect the integrity and confidentiality of sensitive data. By detecting unauthorized access and potential data breaches, IDS helps ensure that critical information remains secure and confidential.

6.7.14. IDS Strengths and Limitations

- **Strengths of Intrusion Detection Systems (IDS):**
  - i. **Real-Time Monitoring:** IDS provides continuous surveillance of network traffic and system activities, allowing for the immediate detection of suspicious behavior. This real-time capability is vital for quick incident response.

ii. **Threat Detection:** IDS can identify a wide range of attacks, including malware infections, unauthorized access attempts, and network intrusions. By employing various detection methods, such as signature-based and anomaly-based techniques, IDS can effectively flag malicious activity.

iii. **Incident Response Support:** By generating alerts and detailed reports on detected threats, IDS helps security teams assess incidents and make informed decisions on containment and remediation. This support is essential for minimizing damage and restoring operations quickly.

iv. **Vulnerability Awareness:** IDS can highlight vulnerabilities in a system by analyzing traffic patterns and identifying abnormal behavior. This information allows organizations to proactively address weaknesses before they can be exploited.

v. **Compliance and Auditing:** Many organizations must adhere to regulatory requirements for monitoring and reporting security incidents. IDS can assist in compliance by providing logs and documentation needed for audits, thereby reinforcing organizational accountability.

- **Limitations of Intrusion Detection Systems (IDS):**

i. **False Positives:** One of the most significant challenges of IDS is the potential for false positives, where legitimate activities are incorrectly flagged as threats. High rates of false alarms can overwhelm security teams and lead to alert fatigue, causing real threats to be overlooked.

ii. **False Negatives:** Conversely, IDS may also fail to detect some attacks, particularly those that employ advanced evasion techniques or are tailored to bypass detection systems. This limitation can create a false sense of security.

iii. **Resource Intensive:** Implementing and maintaining an IDS can be resource-intensive. Continuous monitoring requires substantial processing power, network bandwidth, and storage capacity for log data, which can be costly for organizations.

iv. **Limited Contextual Awareness:** While IDS excels at detecting specific threats, it may lack the broader context needed to understand the full scope of an incident. This limitation can hinder effective incident response.

6.8. NETWORK MANAGEMENT

Network management refers to the process of monitoring, maintaining, and optimizing a computer network to ensure its reliability, performance, and security. It encompasses a range of activities and tools designed to manage network resources effectively, ensuring that users and applications can access data and services without disruption.

- Key Components of Network Management:

i. **Network Monitoring:** Continuous monitoring of network performance is crucial for identifying issues before they escalate. Tools and software are used to track metrics such as bandwidth usage, latency, packet loss, and device status. Real-time alerts help administrators respond quickly to potential problems.

ii. **Configuration Management:** This involves managing the settings and configurations of network devices, such as routers, switches, and firewalls. Proper configuration helps ensure that devices operate efficiently and securely. Changes to configurations should be documented and controlled to prevent misconfigurations.

iii. **Fault Management:** Detecting, isolating, and resolving network faults is a critical aspect of network management. Fault management systems automatically identify issues, categorize them, and notify network administrators. Quick resolution minimizes downtime and maintains service availability.

iv. **Performance Management:** This component focuses on optimizing the performance of the network. It involves analyzing performance data to identify bottlenecks, ensuring that resources are allocated efficiently, and implementing quality of service (QoS) policies to prioritize critical applications.

v. **Security Management:** Protecting the network from threats is a vital aspect of network management. This includes implementing firewalls, intrusion detection systems (IDS), and encryption protocols. Regular security audits and updates help safeguard against vulnerabilities.

vi. **Traffic Management:** Effective traffic management ensures that network resources are used optimally. Techniques such as load balancing distribute traffic evenly across servers, preventing any single point from becoming overwhelmed. This improves overall network performance and reliability.

6.8.1. Management to Ensure Service

Effective management is crucial for ensuring that services—whether IT, customer support, or operational—are delivered consistently, reliably, and efficiently. This encompasses a range of strategies and practices that organizations implement to meet service expectations, manage resources effectively, and adapt to changing demands. Below are key components and best practices for managing services to ensure optimal delivery.

1. **Service Level Agreements (SLAs):** Establishing clear Service Level Agreements (SLAs) is fundamental to service management. SLAs define the expected service quality, performance metrics, and responsibilities of both the service provider and the customer. Key elements of SLAs include:
   - i. **Performance Metrics**: These specify measurable indicators of service quality, such as response time, resolution time, and availability.
   - ii. **Penalties and Remedies**: SLAs should outline consequences for failing to meet agreed-upon standards, providing a framework for accountability.
   - iii. **Review and Revision**: Regularly reviewing SLAs helps ensure they remain relevant and aligned with business needs and customer expectations.
2. **Monitoring and Reporting:** Continuous monitoring of service performance is vital for maintaining service quality. This involves:
   - i. **Real-Time Monitoring**: Utilizing tools and technologies to track service performance metrics in real-time helps identify issues before they escalate.
   - ii. **Regular Reporting**: Generating reports on service performance, incidents, and trends provides insights for stakeholders and aids in informed decision-making.
   - iii. **Feedback Mechanisms**: Implementing systems for gathering feedback from users helps identify areas for improvement and enhances customer satisfaction.
3. **Incident Management:** Effective incident management is critical for ensuring service continuity. This process includes:

i. **Incident Detection and Reporting**: Establishing clear protocols for identifying and reporting incidents ensures timely responses.

ii. **Prioritization**: Incidents should be categorized based on their impact and urgency, allowing teams to address the most critical issues first.

iii. **Resolution and Recovery**: A structured approach to resolving incidents helps minimize downtime and restore services quickly. This may involve root cause analysis to prevent recurrence.

4. **Change Management:** Managing changes within an organization is essential to minimize disruptions and ensure service quality. Change management involves:

i. **Change Requests**: Establishing a formal process for submitting and evaluating change requests helps assess potential impacts on services.

ii. **Impact Assessment**: Analyzing the effects of proposed changes on existing services, infrastructure, and user experience ensures informed decision-making.

iii. **Communication and Training**: Communicating changes effectively to all stakeholders and providing necessary training helps users adapt and reduces resistance.

5. **Resource Management:** Effective resource management is crucial for delivering services consistently. This includes:

i. **Capacity Planning**: Anticipating future service demands and ensuring that the necessary resources (e.g., personnel, technology, and budget) are in place is essential for scaling services effectively.

ii. **Utilization Monitoring**: Continuously monitoring resource utilization helps identify inefficiencies and optimize performance.

iii. **Staffing and Skills Development**: Ensuring that staff possess the necessary skills and knowledge is vital for maintaining service quality. Regular training and professional development programs help keep skills updated.

6. **Customer Relationship Management (CRM):** Building strong relationships with customers is critical for ensuring service quality and satisfaction. This involves:

i. **Communication**: Maintaining open lines of communication with customers fosters trust and allows for better understanding of their needs.

ii. **Proactive Engagement**: Engaging with customers proactively—such as through surveys and check-ins—helps identify potential issues and areas for improvement.

iii. **Personalization**: Tailoring services to meet individual customer needs enhances satisfaction and loyalty.

7. **Continuous Improvement:** A commitment to continuous improvement is essential for ensuring long-term service quality. This includes:

    i. **Regular Reviews**: Conducting periodic reviews of service performance, processes, and customer feedback helps identify areas for enhancement.

    ii. **Adopting Best Practices**: Implementing industry best practices, such as ITIL (Information Technology Infrastructure Library) for IT services, helps standardize processes and improve efficiency.

    iii. **Innovation**: Encouraging a culture of innovation allows teams to explore new technologies and methodologies that can enhance service delivery.

Effective management to ensure service involves a multifaceted approach that includes establishing clear SLAs, continuous monitoring, efficient incident and change management, resource optimization, strong customer relationships, and a commitment to continuous improvement. By focusing on these components, organizations can deliver high-quality services that meet customer expectations, adapt to changing demands, and drive long-term success. In an increasingly competitive environment, prioritizing service management not only enhances customer satisfaction but also fosters loyalty and growth.

6.8.2. Security Information and Event Management (SIEM)

Security Information and Event Management (SIEM) is a crucial technology in the field of cybersecurity, designed to provide real-time analysis of security alerts generated by various hardware and software components within an organization's IT infrastructure. By consolidating and analyzing security data from across the enterprise, SIEM helps organizations detect, respond to, and mitigate potential security threats more effectively.

- **Key Components of SIEM:**

i. Data Collection:

– SIEM systems collect data from various sources, including network devices (routers, switches), servers, domain controllers, applications, and endpoints. This data includes logs, events, and alerts, forming a comprehensive view of the security landscape.

– The collection can be done through agents installed on devices or via network-based monitoring, ensuring minimal performance impact while gathering necessary information.

ii. Normalization: Once data is collected, SIEM systems normalize it into a common format. This process allows for efficient analysis, as it ensures consistency in the data structure, making it easier to compare and correlate different log entries from diverse sources.

iii. Correlation: It is one of the most powerful features of SIEM. The system analyzes normalized data to identify patterns or anomalies that may indicate a security incident. By correlating events from different sources, SIEM can uncover complex attack vectors that may not be apparent when examining logs in isolation.

iv. Alerting: When potential threats are identified through correlation rules, the SIEM generates alerts to notify security teams. These alerts can be prioritized based on severity, allowing analysts to focus on the most critical incidents first.

v. Dashboards and Reporting: SIEM solutions often provide customizable dashboards that visualize security data, making it easier for analysts to understand the current security posture. Additionally, reporting capabilities help organizations meet compliance requirements by generating documentation on security events and incidents.

vi. Incident Response: Many SIEM systems integrate with incident response tools, allowing security teams to investigate and respond to alerts efficiently. This can include automating certain response actions, such as blocking an IP address or quarantining a compromised system.

- **Benefits of SIEM:**

i. Enhanced Threat Detection: SIEM significantly improves an organization's ability to detect threats. By correlating data from multiple sources, SIEM can identify sophisticated attacks that might evade traditional security measures.

ii. **Improved Incident Response:** The centralized visibility and real-time alerts provided by SIEM enable security teams to respond quickly to incidents. Faster response times can minimize damage and reduce recovery costs.

iii. **Regulatory Compliance:** Many industries are subject to regulations that require logging and monitoring of security events. SIEM helps organizations meet compliance standards, such as PCI DSS, HIPAA, and GDPR, by providing the necessary logging and reporting capabilities.

iv. **Operational Efficiency:** By automating data collection, normalization, and correlation, SIEM reduces the manual effort required for security monitoring. This allows security analysts to focus on more strategic tasks rather than sifting through vast amounts of raw data.

v. **Threat Intelligence Integration:** Many SIEM solutions can integrate threat intelligence feeds, enhancing the system's ability to identify known threats and vulnerabilities. This helps organizations stay informed about emerging threats and adjust their defenses accordingly.

- **Challenges of SIEM:**

i. **Complexity and Cost:** Implementing and maintaining a SIEM solution can be complex and expensive. Organizations must invest in hardware, software, and skilled personnel to manage the system effectively.

ii. **False Positives:** SIEM systems can generate false positives, where benign activities are incorrectly flagged as threats. High rates of false positives can lead to alert fatigue among security teams, causing genuine threats to be overlooked.

iii. **Data Overload:** The sheer volume of data collected by SIEM can be overwhelming. Without effective filtering and prioritization mechanisms, analysts may struggle to focus on significant threats.

iv. **Skill Shortages:** Effective SIEM management requires skilled cybersecurity professionals who understand how to configure and tune the system properly. The shortage of qualified personnel can hinder an organization's ability to leverage SIEM effectively.

- **Best Practices for SIEM Implementation:**
  i. **Define Clear Objectives:** Before implementing a SIEM solution, organizations should define clear objectives and use cases. This ensures that the SIEM is tailored to meet specific security needs.
  ii. **Prioritize Data Sources:** Not all data is equally valuable. Organizations should prioritize data sources that are most critical to their security posture, such as servers, firewalls, and critical applications.
  iii. **Regularly Tune and Update:** SIEM systems should be regularly tuned to minimize false positives and improve detection accuracy. This includes updating correlation rules, threat intelligence feeds, and system configurations.
  iv. **Training and Skill Development:** Investing in training for security staff is crucial for maximizing the effectiveness of SIEM. Ensuring that team members are well-versed in the SIEM's capabilities enhances the organization's overall security response.
  v. **Integrate with Other Security Tools:** To maximize the effectiveness of SIEM, organizations should integrate it with other security tools, such as endpoint detection and response (EDR) solutions and threat intelligence platforms. This creates a more comprehensive security ecosystem.

Security Information and Event Management (SIEM) is an essential technology for modern cybersecurity strategies. By providing centralized visibility into security events and enabling real-time threat detection and response, SIEM enhances an organization's ability to protect its assets and respond to incidents effectively. Despite its challenges, the benefits of SIEM in improving threat detection, facilitating compliance, and enhancing operational efficiency make it a vital component of any comprehensive security framework. As cyber threats continue to evolve, SIEM will remain an indispensable tool for organizations seeking to safeguard their information systems.

CHAPTER 7

DATABASE SECURITY

Contents

7.1. INTRODUCTION TO DATABASES

Databases are a fundamental component of modern computing, serving as structured repositories for storing, managing, and retrieving data efficiently. As organizations increasingly rely on data-driven decision-making, understanding databases has become essential across various fields, from business to healthcare and beyond. At its core, a database is designed to organize data in a way that facilitates easy access and manipulation. Traditional relational databases, built on a structured framework of tables, rows, and columns, utilize the Structured

Query Language (SQL) for querying and managing data. This model ensures data integrity, supports complex queries, and allows for relationships between different data entities through primary and foreign keys. With the advent of big data, NoSQL databases have gained prominence, offering flexibility and scalability to handle unstructured and semi-structured data. These databases, such as MongoDB and Cassandra, cater to specific needs such as high-volume transactions and real-time analytics, making them ideal for applications like social media and IoT systems. Database management systems (DBMS) play a critical role in maintaining databases, providing tools for data modeling, backup, recovery, and security. They enable multiple users to interact with the database concurrently while ensuring data consistency and integrity. As the demand for data continues to grow, advancements in database technologies, such as cloud databases and distributed database systems, are reshaping how organizations store and access information. These innovations facilitate seamless integration, enhance performance, and support the scalability required for modern applications. Databases are integral to the effective management of information in today's digital landscape. A solid understanding of database concepts and technologies is essential for anyone looking to navigate the complexities of data management in various domains.

7.1.1. Concept of a Database

A database is a structured collection of data that allows for efficient storage, retrieval, and management. It organizes information in a way that facilitates easy access and manipulation, typically through a Database Management System (DBMS). The most common type is the relational database, which uses tables to represent data and establishes relationships between them using keys. Databases support various operations, such as querying, updating, and reporting, through languages like SQL. They ensure data integrity, consistency, and security, enabling multiple users to interact with the data concurrently. With the rise of big data, NoSQL databases have emerged to handle unstructured and semi-structured data, offering greater flexibility and scalability. Overall, databases are crucial for modern applications, underpinning everything from business operations to web services, and are essential for effective data management in diverse fields.

7.1.2. Components of Databases

Databases consist of several key components that work together to facilitate data storage, management, and retrieval. Understanding these components is essential for effective database design and operation.

1. **Database Management System (DBMS):** The core software that manages databases. It provides the tools needed for creating, updating, and querying data. Common DBMSs include MySQL, Oracle, and Microsoft SQL Server. They ensure data integrity, security, and concurrency control.
2. **Data Model:** This defines how data is structured and organized. The most prevalent model is the relational model, which organizes data into tables with rows and columns. Other models include NoSQL databases (document, key-value, graph) that accommodate different data types and usage patterns.
3. **Schema:** A blueprint of the database that defines the structure, including tables, fields, relationships, and constraints. The schema dictates how data is organized and how entities interact, ensuring consistency and integrity.
4. **Tables:** In relational databases, data is stored in tables, which consist of rows (records) and columns (attributes). Each table represents a specific entity, such as customers or orders.
5. **Keys:** Keys are essential for establishing relationships between tables. A primary key uniquely identifies each record within a table, while foreign keys link records from one table to another, enforcing referential integrity.
6. **Queries:** These are requests for data retrieval or manipulation. SQL is the standard language used for writing queries, allowing users to select, insert, update, and delete data.
7. **Data Storage:** The physical storage where data resides, often managed by the DBMS. This includes files, indexes, and data structures that optimize access speed and storage efficiency.
8. **User Interface:** Tools and applications that allow users to interact with the database, ranging from command-line interfaces to graphical user interfaces (GUIs).

Together, these components create a cohesive system that enables efficient data management, ensuring that information is accessible, reliable, and secure.

7.1.3. Advantages of Using Databases

Databases offer numerous advantages that make them essential for managing data effectively in various applications:

1. **Data Integrity and Consistency:** Databases enforce rules and constraints, ensuring that data remains accurate and consistent. This reduces the risk of data anomalies and improves overall data quality.

2. **Efficient Data Management:** With structured organization, databases allow for quick and efficient data retrieval and manipulation. Users can perform complex queries, update records, and generate reports with ease.
3. **Scalability:** Databases can handle increasing amounts of data and user requests. Modern database systems, particularly cloud-based solutions, can scale resources dynamically to meet growing demands.
4. **Concurrent Access:** Multiple users can access and manipulate data simultaneously without conflicts, thanks to built-in concurrency controls. This is crucial for collaborative environments and applications.
5. **Security:** Databases offer robust security features, including user authentication and authorization, encryption, and backup options. This protects sensitive data from unauthorized access and breaches.
6. **Data Redundancy Minimization:** Databases reduce data duplication by using normalized structures, which leads to more efficient storage and easier data management.
7. **Backup and Recovery:** Most database systems provide automated backup and recovery options, ensuring data can be restored in case of corruption or loss.
8. **Support for Data Relationships:** Databases facilitate complex relationships between different data entities, allowing for comprehensive data analysis and reporting.

Overall, these advantages make databases a vital tool for organizations aiming to leverage data for informed decision-making and operational efficiency.

7.2. SECURITY REQUIREMENTS OF DATABASES

Security is paramount in database management, as databases often contain sensitive and critical information. Key security requirements include:

1. **Access Control:** Implementing robust access control mechanisms ensures that only authorized users can access the database. This includes user authentication (verifying identities) and authorization (granting permissions based on roles).
2. **Data Encryption:** Encrypting data both at rest and in transit protects it from unauthorized access. Encryption ensures that even if data is intercepted or accessed, it remains unreadable without the proper decryption keys.

3. **Auditing and Monitoring:** Regularly auditing database activities helps detect unauthorized access or anomalies. Continuous monitoring allows for the timely identification of suspicious behavior, enabling rapid responses to potential threats.
4. **Data Integrity:** Maintaining data integrity involves protecting against unauthorized modifications. Techniques like checksums and digital signatures can help verify the accuracy and authenticity of data.
5. **Backup and Recovery:** Establishing a reliable backup and recovery plan ensures that data can be restored in the event of corruption, loss, or security breaches. Regular backups protect against data loss and provide a way to recover compromised data.
6. **Security Patches and Updates:** Keeping the database management system and related software updated with the latest security patches is crucial for protecting against vulnerabilities and exploits.
7. **Compliance with Regulations:** Adhering to legal and regulatory requirements, such as GDPR or HIPAA, ensures that sensitive data is handled appropriately, protecting both the organization and its users.

By addressing these security requirements, organizations can significantly enhance the protection of their databases and safeguard sensitive information from evolving threats.

7.2.1. Integrity of the Database

The integrity of a database is essential for ensuring the accuracy, consistency, and reliability of the data it contains. Maintaining database integrity involves several key principles:

1. **Entity Integrity:** This principle ensures that each table has a unique primary key, which uniquely identifies each record. By enforcing entity integrity, databases prevent duplicate entries and guarantee that each record is distinct.
2. **Referential Integrity:** This aspect maintains valid relationships between tables through the use of foreign keys. It ensures that foreign key values correspond to existing primary keys in related tables, preventing orphaned records and ensuring data consistency across the database.
3. **Domain Integrity:** Domain integrity enforces constraints on the types of data that can be stored in each column of a table. This includes restrictions on data types, ranges, and formats, ensuring that only valid and appropriate data is entered.

4. **User-Defined Integrity:** Organizations can implement specific rules and constraints that reflect business requirements. This may include custom validation rules enforced through triggers or application logic, ensuring that the data adheres to organizational standards.
5. **Concurrency Control:** In environments where multiple users access the database simultaneously, concurrency control mechanisms (like locking) help prevent conflicts and maintain integrity during concurrent transactions.

By prioritizing these integrity measures, organizations can safeguard their databases against errors, inconsistencies, and data corruption, ensuring that the information remains trustworthy and valuable for decision-making and reporting. Ultimately, maintaining database integrity is crucial for operational efficiency and data-driven insights.

7.2.2. Element Integrity

Element integrity, often referred to as domain integrity, is a critical aspect of database management that ensures the accuracy and validity of data stored within individual fields or columns. This concept involves enforcing specific constraints and rules that dictate what type of data can be entered into each element of a database table.

1. **Data Types:** Each column in a table is assigned a specific data type (e.g., integer, string, date) that defines the nature of the data allowed. This prevents inappropriate data entries, such as entering text in a numerical field.
2. **Constraints:** Various constraints can be applied to enforce element integrity, including:
   - i. **NOT NULL:** Ensures that a field cannot have a null value, requiring that every record must contain a value.
   - ii. **UNIQUE:** Guarantees that all values in a column are distinct, preventing duplicates.
   - iii. **CHECK:** Allows for custom conditions to validate data. For example, a CHECK constraint can enforce that a numerical field must be greater than zero.
3. **Default Values:** Element integrity can also be maintained by setting default values for certain fields, ensuring that even if no value is provided during data entry, a valid default will be applied.

By enforcing element integrity, databases enhance data quality, reduce the likelihood of errors, and ensure that only valid and meaningful information is stored. This is vital for effective data analysis and reporting, as accurate data underpins informed decision-making within organizations. Ultimately, element integrity contributes to the overall reliability and trustworthiness of a database system.

7.2.3. Auditability

Auditability in databases refers to the ability to track and record all activities and changes made to data within the system. This feature is crucial for ensuring accountability, compliance, and security, making it a fundamental aspect of effective database management.

1. **Change Tracking:** Auditability enables organizations to monitor alterations to data, including who made the changes, when they were made, and the nature of those changes. This tracking is essential for identifying unauthorized modifications or data breaches.
2. **Log Files:** Many database systems maintain detailed log files that record transactions and activities. These logs can capture actions such as data insertions, updates, deletions, and user logins, providing a comprehensive history of database interactions.
3. **Compliance and Regulations:** Many industries are subject to regulations that require audit trails for data management practices. For instance, regulations like GDPR and HIPAA mandate organizations to maintain records of data access and changes to ensure compliance and protect sensitive information.
4. **Incident Investigation:** In the event of a security incident or data breach, audit logs are invaluable for forensic investigations. They help trace back to the source of the breach, assess the extent of the damage, and implement corrective measures.
5. **Performance Monitoring:** Auditable systems also allow organizations to analyze usage patterns and performance metrics, enabling better resource allocation and optimization.

By incorporating robust auditability features, organizations enhance their ability to maintain data integrity, ensure compliance, and strengthen their overall security posture, fostering trust in their data management practices.

7.2.4. Access Control

Access control is a fundamental aspect of database security that regulates who can view or modify data within a database system. By implementing robust access control mechanisms, organizations can protect sensitive information and ensure that only authorized users have access to specific data.

1. **User Authentication:** The first line of defense in access control is user authentication, which verifies the identity of individuals trying to access the database. This can involve methods such as usernames and passwords, biometric scans, or multi-factor authentication, enhancing security by requiring multiple verification steps.
2. **Authorization:** Once a user is authenticated, authorization determines their level of access based on predefined roles and permissions. Role-Based Access Control (RBAC) is commonly used, where users are assigned roles that dictate their access rights, ensuring that individuals can only perform actions relevant to their responsibilities.
3. **Granular Permissions:** Access control can be fine-tuned to provide granular permissions, allowing different users to have varying levels of access to specific tables, columns, or even individual records. This minimizes the risk of unauthorized data exposure.
4. **Audit Trails:** Monitoring access attempts and actions taken within the database is vital for maintaining security. Audit trails help track who accessed what data and when, enabling organizations to identify and respond to suspicious activities.
5. **Regular Review and Updates:** Regularly reviewing access controls and permissions is essential to adapt to changes in personnel, roles, and organizational needs. This proactive approach helps maintain a secure database environment.

7.2.5. User Authentication

User authentication is a critical component of database security, ensuring that only authorized individuals can access sensitive information. It involves verifying the identity of users before granting them access to a database system. Here are the key elements of user authentication:

1. **Authentication Methods:** Various methods can be employed for user authentication, including:
   - i. **Username and Password:** The most common method, where users provide a unique identifier (username) and a secret (password). Strong password policies are essential to enhance security.
   - ii. **Multi-Factor Authentication (MFA):** This method adds an extra layer of security by requiring users to provide two or

more verification factors, such as a password and a one-time code sent to their mobile device.

iii. **Biometric Authentication:** Techniques such as fingerprint scanning, facial recognition, or iris scans provide a high level of security by using unique physical characteristics.

2. **Session Management:** Once authenticated, user sessions must be managed effectively. This includes setting timeouts for inactive sessions and requiring re-authentication for sensitive operations.
3. **Access Controls:** After authentication, the system enforces access controls based on the user's role, ensuring that individuals can only access data pertinent to their responsibilities.
4. **Password Policies:** Implementing strong password policies, including complexity requirements and regular password changes, helps mitigate the risk of unauthorized access.
5. **Audit and Monitoring:** Regularly monitoring authentication attempts and maintaining logs of access activities can help identify and respond to suspicious behavior.

In conclusion, robust user authentication is essential for protecting database systems against unauthorized access, thereby safeguarding sensitive data and maintaining overall security.

7.2.6. Availability

Availability in database management refers to the capacity of a database to remain accessible and operational when needed. It is crucial for ensuring that users can retrieve and manipulate data without interruptions. Key factors affecting availability include:

1. **Redundancy:** Implementing redundant systems, such as database replication and clustering, enhances availability by providing alternative data sources in case of hardware failures.
2. **Backup and Recovery:** Regular backups and well-defined recovery procedures are essential for restoring data quickly after an incident, minimizing downtime.
3. **Load Balancing:** Distributing workloads across multiple servers helps prevent any single point of failure, ensuring that resources remain available during peak usage times.
4. **Maintenance and Monitoring:** Routine maintenance, combined with proactive monitoring, allows for the early detection of issues that could affect availability, enabling timely intervention.

7.2.7. Integrity/Confidentiality/Availability

Integrity, confidentiality, and availability—often referred to as the CIA triad—are foundational principles of information security, particularly in database management.

Integrity ensures that data remains accurate, consistent, and trustworthy throughout its lifecycle. It involves implementing mechanisms such as primary keys, foreign keys, and constraints to prevent unauthorized modifications or corruption of data. By maintaining integrity, organizations can rely on the quality of their data for decision-making and operational processes.

Confidentiality protects sensitive information from unauthorized access and disclosure. This is achieved through various security measures, including user authentication, encryption, and access control mechanisms. Ensuring confidentiality is vital for safeguarding personal and proprietary information, particularly in industries like healthcare and finance, where data breaches can have serious consequences.

Availability refers to the assurance that data and resources are accessible to authorized users when needed. High availability is critical for business continuity, requiring strategies such as redundancy, load balancing, and failover systems to minimize downtime. Organizations must also conduct regular maintenance to ensure their systems remain operational and responsive.

Together, these principles create a comprehensive security framework that protects data from threats, ensuring it remains reliable, private, and accessible. Prioritizing the CIA triad helps organizations maintain trust with stakeholders and comply with regulatory requirements, ultimately enhancing overall security posture.

7.3. RELIABILITY AND INTEGRITY

Reliability and integrity are essential attributes in database management, playing crucial roles in ensuring the trustworthiness and availability of data.

Reliability refers to the ability of a database to consistently perform its intended functions without failure. A reliable database ensures that data is accessible and operational at all times, minimizing downtime and disruptions. To achieve reliability, organizations often implement redundancy, such as backup systems and data replication. These strategies ensure that, in the event of a failure, alternative systems can take over seamlessly, preserving continuous access to data. Regular maintenance and monitoring also contribute to a database's reliability by identifying potential issues before they escalate.

Integrity, on the other hand, ensures the accuracy and consistency of data within the database. It involves enforcing rules and constraints, such as primary keys and foreign keys, to prevent unauthorized changes and maintain data quality. Integrity mechanisms help detect and correct errors, ensuring that the data remains valid and trustworthy over time. Regular audits and validation checks further support data integrity by identifying discrepancies and enforcing data governance policies.

Together, reliability and integrity create a robust framework for managing data. While reliability ensures that data is consistently available, integrity guarantees that it remains accurate and trustworthy. Organizations that prioritize these attributes can better support decision-making processes, enhance operational efficiency, and maintain the confidence of their stakeholders, ultimately contributing to successful business outcomes.

7.3.1. Protection Features from the Operating System

Operating systems (OS) play a crucial role in protecting data and ensuring the security of databases and applications. Various protection features built into modern operating systems help safeguard against unauthorized access, data breaches, and other vulnerabilities. Here are some key protection features:

1. **User Authentication:** Operating systems require users to authenticate their identities through methods such as passwords, biometrics, or multi-factor authentication. This ensures that only authorized users can access the system and its resources.
2. **Access Control Mechanisms:** OSs implement access control lists (ACLs) and permissions to manage user access to files and resources. These controls specify who can read, write, or execute files, thus preventing unauthorized modifications and ensuring that users can only access data relevant to their roles.
3. **File System Security:** Modern operating systems use advanced file systems that incorporate security features such as encryption and integrity checks. This protects data at rest by ensuring that even if physical access is gained, unauthorized users cannot read or alter the data without proper credentials.
4. **Process Isolation:** The OS enforces process isolation, meaning that each application runs in its own protected memory space. This prevents one process from interfering with another, reducing the risk of malicious software affecting the overall system stability or accessing sensitive data from other applications.

5. **Audit and Logging:** Operating systems maintain logs of user activities, access attempts, and system changes. This auditing capability allows administrators to monitor for suspicious activities and investigate incidents, enhancing accountability and providing insights into potential security breaches.
6. **Security Updates and Patch Management:** Regular updates from operating system vendors address known vulnerabilities and bugs. Effective patch management ensures that systems are equipped with the latest security enhancements, minimizing the risk of exploitation by attackers.
7. **Firewall and Intrusion Detection Systems (IDS):** Operating systems often include built-in firewalls and may support IDS to monitor and control incoming and outgoing network traffic, protecting the system from unauthorized access and potential threats.

By leveraging these protection features, operating systems provide a foundational layer of security that is essential for safeguarding data and maintaining the integrity of database systems and applications.

7.3.2. Two-Phase Update

The Two-Phase Update protocol is a critical technique used in database management systems to ensure consistency and integrity during concurrent transactions. This protocol consists of two distinct phases: the growing phase and the shrinking phase.

1. **Growing Phase:** In this initial phase, a transaction can acquire locks on the data it needs to access, preventing other transactions from making conflicting changes. During this phase, the transaction can continue to request additional locks but cannot release any locks. This ensures that all necessary resources are secured before any modifications are made.
2. **Shrinking Phase:** Once the transaction has completed all necessary operations, it enters the shrinking phase, where it begins to release the locks, it acquired. At this stage, no new locks can be obtained. This ensures that once a transaction starts releasing its locks, it is committed to completing its operations, thus maintaining data consistency.

The Two-Phase Update protocol prevents issues such as dirty reads, lost updates, and inconsistent data states. By ensuring that a transaction either fully completes or is completely rolled back, it enhances the reliability of database transactions. This protocol is particularly important in environments with high concurrency, where multiple transactions may be accessing and modifying the same data simultaneously, safeguarding the integrity and consistency of the database.

7.3.3. Redundancy/Internal Consistency

Redundancy and internal consistency are essential concepts in database management that contribute to data integrity and reliability.

Redundancy refers to the duplication of data within a database system to enhance availability and fault tolerance. While it may seem counterintuitive to have multiple copies of the same data, redundancy can be beneficial. For instance, in distributed databases or systems that require high availability, redundant copies ensure that if one node fails, others can provide access to the same information, minimizing downtime. However, excessive redundancy can lead to challenges such as increased storage costs and data synchronization issues, which need to be managed effectively.

Internal consistency, on the other hand, ensures that all data within the database adheres to predefined rules and constraints. This concept is crucial for maintaining data integrity. For example, in a relational database, foreign key constraints ensure that relationships between tables are consistent. If a record in one table references a record in another table, internal consistency guarantees that the referenced record exists.

To maintain internal consistency, databases often employ mechanisms like transactions, which bundle multiple operations into a single unit of work. If any part of the transaction fails, the entire operation is rolled back, preserving the database's state.

In summary, while redundancy enhances data availability, internal consistency safeguards the accuracy and integrity of that data. Together, these concepts from a balanced approach to data management, ensuring that databases are both resilient and trustworthy.

7.3.4. Recovery

Recovery in database management refers to the processes and mechanisms used to restore a database to a consistent state after a failure, corruption, or data loss. Effective recovery is crucial for maintaining data integrity and availability, ensuring that users can access reliable information even in adverse situations.

There are two primary types of recovery methods:

1. **Backups:** Regularly creating backup copies of the database is essential. These backups can be full, incremental, or differential,

depending on the organization's needs. In the event of data loss due to hardware failure, accidental deletion, or corruption, the database can be restored from the most recent backup, minimizing data loss.

2. **Transaction Logging:** Most modern databases utilize transaction logs to track changes made to the data. These logs record every transaction and its state, enabling recovery processes to replay transactions up to a specific point in time. This method ensures that any committed transactions are preserved, while uncommitted ones can be rolled back, maintaining consistency.

Recovery strategies also include failover mechanisms that switch operations to a standby system in case of primary system failure, ensuring continuous availability.

Overall, effective recovery planning involves implementing both backup and logging strategies, regular testing of recovery processes, and maintaining up-to-date documentation. This comprehensive approach minimizes downtime, protects data integrity, and enhances user trust in the database system.

7.3.5. Concurrency/Consistency

Concurrency and consistency are fundamental concepts in database management that address how multiple transactions interact with each other while maintaining data integrity.

Concurrency refers to the ability of a database to handle multiple transactions simultaneously. In environments where numerous users access the database at the same time, concurrency control mechanisms are essential to ensure that transactions do not interfere with each other. Without proper controls, issues like lost updates, dirty reads, and phantom reads can arise. Common concurrency control methods include locking mechanisms, where transactions acquire locks on data items before accessing them, and timestamp ordering, which assigns a unique timestamp to each transaction to determine the order of operations.

Consistency, on the other hand, ensures that a database remains in a valid state before and after a transaction is executed. When a transaction is completed, it must leave the database in a consistent state, adhering to all predefined rules, constraints, and business logic. For instance, in a banking application, a transfer of funds from one account to another must ensure that the total balance remains the same before and after the transaction.

To maintain both concurrency and consistency, databases often implement the ACID properties (Atomicity, Consistency, Isolation, Durability). These properties ensure that transactions are processed reliably, maintaining data integrity even in the presence of concurrent operations.

In summary, effective concurrency control mechanisms are vital for enabling multiple transactions to execute simultaneously, while consistency ensures that data remains accurate and valid, safeguarding the overall integrity of the database system.

7.4. DATABASE DISCLOSURE

Database disclosure refers to the unauthorized exposure of sensitive data stored within a database. This issue poses significant risks to organizations, including loss of customer trust, legal ramifications, and financial penalties. Data disclosure can occur due to various factors, including security breaches, inadequate access controls, and human error.

1. **Types of Data Disclosed:** Sensitive information can include personal identifiable information (PII), financial records, health data, trade secrets, and other proprietary information. The impact of such disclosures can be severe, particularly in industries like healthcare and finance, where regulatory compliance is critical.
2. **Causes of Disclosure:** Common causes include cyberattacks, such as SQL injection or phishing attacks, which exploit vulnerabilities to gain unauthorized access. Misconfigured databases or weak authentication practices can also lead to exposure. Additionally, accidental disclosures can occur through human error, such as misplacing sensitive files or inadvertently sending data to the wrong recipient.
3. **Preventive Measures:** To mitigate the risk of database disclosure, organizations should implement robust security measures, including strong access controls, regular audits, encryption of sensitive data, and employee training on data handling practices. Intrusion detection systems can also help identify potential breaches in real-time.
4. **Incident Response:** In the event of a disclosure, having an incident response plan is crucial. This includes identifying the source of the breach, notifying affected individuals, and taking corrective measures to prevent future occurrences.

7.4.1. Sensitive Data

Sensitive data refers to any information that must be protected to ensure the privacy and security of individuals or organizations. This type of data, if disclosed or accessed without authorization, can lead to significant harm, including identity theft, financial loss, and reputational damage.

1. **Types of Sensitive Data:** Common categories include:
   i. **Personal Identifiable Information (PII):** This includes names, addresses, Social Security numbers, and phone numbers. Such information can be used to identify individuals and is often targeted by cybercriminals.
   ii. **Financial Information:** Data such as bank account numbers, credit card information, and transaction histories are critical for financial security and must be safeguarded.
   iii. **Health Information:** Medical records, health insurance information, and other related data are considered highly sensitive due to their personal nature and are protected under regulations like HIPAA.
   iv. **Trade Secrets:** Proprietary information, formulas, and business strategies are vital for maintaining competitive advantage and must be protected from corporate espionage.
2. **Protection Measures:** Organizations must implement strong security measures to protect sensitive data. This includes data encryption, access controls, regular security audits, and employee training on data protection best practices. Compliance with regulations such as GDPR and CCPA is also essential to ensure that sensitive data is handled appropriately.
3. **Consequences of Breaches:** Unauthorized access to sensitive data can lead to severe consequences, including legal penalties, loss of customer trust, and financial liabilities. Thus, protecting sensitive data is not just a regulatory requirement but a critical aspect of maintaining an organization's integrity and reputation.

7.4.2. Types of Disclosures

Types of disclosures refer to the various ways sensitive or confidential information can be unintentionally or intentionally revealed. Understanding these types is crucial for organizations to implement effective data protection strategies.

1. **Unauthorized Disclosure:** This occurs when individuals gain access to sensitive data without permission. It can result from cyberattacks, such as hacking or phishing, where attackers exploit vulnerabilities to access confidential information.
2. **Accidental Disclosure:** Sensitive data can be inadvertently exposed due to human error. Examples include sending an email to the wrong

recipient, misplacing physical documents, or improperly configuring databases that allow public access to sensitive information.

3. **Regulatory Disclosure:** Organizations may be required to disclose certain data to comply with legal or regulatory obligations. This includes reporting breaches to authorities or providing information during audits. While these disclosures are legitimate, they can still expose sensitive data if not managed carefully.
4. **Public Disclosure:** In some cases, organizations may choose to disclose information publicly, such as during press releases or financial reports. While this can enhance transparency, it must be handled carefully to avoid unintentionally revealing sensitive details.
5. **Social Engineering Disclosure:** This occurs when individuals manipulate employees into revealing confidential information. Techniques include impersonating IT staff or using psychological tricks to gain trust.

7.4.3. Preventing Disclosure: Data Suppression and Modification

Preventing data disclosure is essential for protecting sensitive information, and two effective strategies are data suppression and modification.

Data Suppression involves removing or obscuring sensitive information before it is shared or analyzed. This technique ensures that critical data, such as personal identifiable information (PII) or confidential business details, is not exposed during processes like reporting or data sharing. For example, in a dataset containing employee information, names and social security numbers can be suppressed to prevent unauthorized access while still allowing analysis of non-sensitive attributes, such as job roles or salaries. Data suppression helps organizations comply with regulations like GDPR and HIPAA, which mandate the protection of personal data.

Data Modification refers to altering sensitive data to protect its confidentiality while maintaining its usability. Techniques like anonymization or pseudonymization transform identifiable information into a format that cannot be traced back to the individual. For instance, replacing names with unique identifiers allows data analysis without compromising individual identities. While modification maintains the data's integrity for analytical purposes, it minimizes the risk of exposure.

Implementing these strategies requires a thorough understanding of the data being handled and the potential risks associated with its disclosure. Organizations should also ensure that employees are trained in best practices for data handling, reinforcing the importance of safeguarding sensitive information.

By employing data suppression and modification techniques, organizations can significantly reduce the risk of unauthorized disclosures, ensuring compliance with legal requirements and protecting the privacy of individuals and sensitive business information.

7.4.4. Security versus Precision

Security and precision are two critical yet often conflicting aspects of data management, particularly in the context of database systems and information processing. Security refers to the measures taken to protect data from unauthorized access, breaches, and other threats. High levels of security are essential for safeguarding sensitive information, such as personal identifiable information (PII) and financial data. Implementing strong encryption, access controls, and regular audits enhances security but can also complicate data retrieval and processing.

Precision, on the other hand, involves the accuracy and correctness of data. High precision ensures that data is reliable and can be used effectively for decision-making, analysis, and reporting. In environments where data accuracy is paramount, such as healthcare or financial sectors, maintaining precision is crucial. However, stringent security measures, such as anonymization or data suppression, can sometimes reduce the level of detail and granularity of data, impacting its precision.

The tension between security and precision arises when organizations must balance these two priorities. For example, while encrypting sensitive data enhances security, it may complicate access for legitimate users, potentially leading to delays or errors in data processing. Conversely, prioritizing precision might expose sensitive data to security vulnerabilities.

To achieve a harmonious balance, organizations can implement role-based access controls, ensuring that users have access to the data they need without compromising security. Regularly assessing the risks and benefits of security measures against the need for precision allows organizations to maintain data integrity while effectively protecting sensitive information. Ultimately, finding this balance is vital for effective data management and operational success.

7.5. DATA MINING AND BIG DATA

The exponential growth of digital data has given rise to the era of Big Data characterized by its volume, velocity, variety, veracity, and value. In the context of computational security, Big Data presents both a challenge and an opportunity. The challenge lies in processing and securing massive and diverse datasets in real time. The opportunity, however, is the potential to extract valuable insights using data mining techniques to enhance threat detection, prediction, and response mechanisms. Data mining refers to the process of discovering patterns, correlations, and anomalies in large datasets using statistical, machine learning, and AI-based techniques. In security, data mining enables proactive defense mechanisms by identifying emerging threats, insider risks, and behavioral anomalies. For example, clustering algorithms can detect unusual login patterns that may signify a brute-force attack, while classification models can be trained to distinguish between normal and malicious network traffic.

When integrated with Big Data platforms (e.g., Hadoop, Spark), data mining scales to handle petabytes of data across distributed systems. This is especially critical for security operations centers (SOCs), which rely on real-time analytics from diverse sources—such as logs, sensors, social media, and threat intelligence feeds. The fusion of data mining with Big Data facilitates advanced applications like Security Information and Event Management (SIEM), User and Entity Behavior Analytics (UEBA), and automated threat hunting.

However, leveraging data mining in Big Data security also introduces privacy and ethical concerns. Mining sensitive user data can lead to unintentional breaches of confidentiality, especially if access controls and anonymization measures are inadequate. Furthermore, the accuracy of data mining outputs depends heavily on data quality and bias-free training sets.

Data mining and Big Data are indispensable to modern computational security. When effectively combined, they empower organizations to move from reactive to predictive security postures. As cyber threats become more sophisticated, scalable data analysis techniques will continue to be essential tools for securing complex digital ecosystems.

PRACTICAL EXPERIMENTS

EXPERIMENT 1: UNDERSTANDING THREATS AND CONTROLS

- Objective: The purpose of this experiment is to help students understand the foundational concepts of computer security, specifically the relationships between assets, threats, vulnerabilities, and controls.
- **Procedure:**
  - Begin by identifying various digital assets in your personal computer or college lab system. Examples include documents, passwords, pictures, emails, and financial data.
  - List out possible threats that could compromise these assets. For example, threats to confidentiality (unauthorized access), integrity (unauthorized changes), and availability (denial of access).
  - Next, analyze potential vulnerabilities in the system such as outdated software, lack of password protection, or no encryption.
  - Finally, suggest suitable security controls for each identified threat. Examples include antivirus software, firewalls, strong passwords, data backups, and access control mechanisms.
- **Outcome:** By the end of this practical, students will understand how to map real-world scenarios into the security triad model:

Confidentiality, Integrity, and Availability (CIA). They will also understand the importance of identifying and prioritizing threats and implementing appropriate countermeasures.

- Tools Required:
  - Pen & Paper or Spreadsheet (Excel or Google Sheets)
  - Internet access (optional for research)

EXPERIMENT 2: IMPLEMENTING MULTIFACTOR AUTHENTICATION (MFA)

- Objective: To configure and experience the working of a multifactor authentication (MFA) system using real-world applications.
- Procedure: Log in to a web service that supports MFA such as Google, GitHub, or Microsoft. First, ensure that your primary login (username and password) is functional. Then, access account security settings and enable MFA or two-factor authentication (2FA).

  You will be prompted to choose a second authentication factor. Select a mobile authenticator app like Google Authenticator or Authy. Scan the QR code displayed on the website using the app. The app will begin generating time-based one-time passwords (TOTP) every 30 seconds.

  Now test the login process by logging out and trying to sign back in. The system will now require both your password and a verification code from the authenticator app. Explore additional MFA options such as SMS-based codes or backup codes.
- **Expected Outcome:** Understand how MFA improves system security by adding an extra layer of identity verification, making it more difficult for attackers to gain unauthorized access.
- **Tools Required:**
  - A personal device with internet access
  - Authenticator app (Google Authenticator, Microsoft Authenticator, etc.).

EXPERIMENT 3: FILE ENCRYPTION AND DECRYPTION USING OPENSSL

- **Objective:** To perform file encryption and decryption using OpenSSL and understand basic cryptographic operations.

- **Procedure:** Install OpenSSL if it's not already present. Create a simple text file (e.g., message.txt) and write confidential information inside it. Use OpenSSL to generate an RSA key pair:
  - openssl genpkey -algorithm RSA -out private.pem
  - openssl rsa -in private.pem -pubout -out public.pem
  - Now, encrypt the message using the public key:
  - openssl rsautl -encrypt -inkey public.pem -pubin -in message.txt -out encrypted.bin
  - Decrypt the encrypted file using the private key:
  - openssl rsautl -decrypt -inkey private.pem -in encrypted.bin -out decrypted.txt

Compare decrypted.txt with the original message file to verify successful decryption.

- **Expected Outcome:** User will gain an understanding of asymmetric encryption, the use of public/private key pairs, and practical encryption/decryption using real tools.
- **Tools Required:**
  - OpenSSL installed (Linux, Windows, or macOS)
  - Terminal or command prompt

EXPERIMENT 4: SIMULATE BUFFER OVERFLOW IN C

- **Objective:** To demonstrate a buffer overflow vulnerability and understand how it can lead to system crashes or security breaches.
- Procedure: Write a simple C program that takes user input into a fixed-size buffer without checking its length.

```
#include <stdio.h>
void main() {
char buffer[10];
printf("Enter your input: ");
gets(buffer);
printf("You entered: %s\n," buffer);
}
```

Compile and run the program. Enter input longer than 10 characters and observe how the program behaves. It may crash or show undefined behavior due to memory overflow.

Now fix the program by replacing gets(buffer) with fgets(buffer, sizeof(buffer), stdin); and test again.

- **Expected Outcome:** Understand how buffer overflow occurs and how input validation and boundary checks can prevent it.
- **Tools Required:**
  - C compiler (GCC)
  - Linux or Windows environment

EXPERIMENT 5: MALWARE STATIC ANALYSIS WITH VIRUSTOTAL

- **Objective:** To perform basic static malware analysis using online tools like VirusTotal and learn how antivirus engines detect threats.
- **Procedure:** Find a benign executable file (or use a known test virus file like the EICAR test file, which is harmless). Visit https://www.virustotal.com and upload the file.

Once uploaded, VirusTotal scans the file using multiple antivirus engines (like Kaspersky, BitDefender, Avast, etc.). Observe:

- Detection names from different engines
- File behavior (e.g., registry access, network activity)
- Metadata like file type, size, hash values

Also explore the "Behavior" and "Community" tabs to see if users have commented on similar files.

- **Expected Outcome:** Understand how multiple security vendors detect and classify threats. Learn about file hashes, suspicious indicators, and how community-based feedback contributes to malware identification.
- **Tools Required:**
  - Internet browser
  - VirusTotal account (optional for more features)
  - Test file (e.g., EICAR)

EXPERIMENT 6: CROSS-SITE SCRIPTING (XSS) DEMO

- **Objective:** To simulate a basic Cross-Site Scripting (XSS) attack and then fix the vulnerability using input validation.
- **Procedure:** Create a simple HTML form that accepts a comment and displays it back to the user:

```
<form method="GET">
Enter comment: <input name="comment">
<input type="submit">
</form>
<p>Your comment: <?php echo $_GET["comment"]; ?></p>
```

Save the file as xss_demo.php and host it using XAMPP or WAMP. In the comment box, enter:

```
<script>alert('XSS');</script>
```

If an alert box pops up, the site is vulnerable to XSS. Now apply basic input sanitization using htmlspecialchars() in PHP:

```
echo htmlspecialchars($_GET["comment"]);
```

Expected Outcome:

Understand how JavaScript can be injected and executed through user input and how to prevent it via sanitization.

- **Tools Required:**
  - XAMPP/WAMP (local server)
  - Basic PHP and HTML knowledge

EXPERIMENT 7: EMAIL HEADER ANALYSIS FOR PHISHING DETECTION

- **Objective:** To analyze raw email headers to identify phishing attempts and understand how email spoofing works.
- **Procedure:** Open your email client (Gmail, Outlook, etc.) and find a suspicious or spam email. Click on "Show Original" or "View Source" to access the email headers.

Check for the following fields:

- Received: chain – Check if the email came from an unknown or suspicious IP

- From: address – Does it match the actual sender?
- SPF/DKIM/DMARC results – Are they marked as "pass" or "fail"?
- Any discrepancies in the "Return-Path" or "Reply-To" fields

Compare the visible sender and technical sender. Use tools like MXToolbox to verify domain authenticity.

- **Expected Outcome:** Understand how phishing works at the header level and how attackers spoof sender identities. Learn to verify email legitimacy before clicking on links or attachments.
- **Tools Required:**
  - Email account with access to full headers
  - Online DNS lookup tools

EXPERIMENT 8: CONFIGURE A FIREWALL USING IPTABLES OR WINDOWS DEFENDER

- **Objective:** To set up basic firewall rules to allow or block specific services and monitor the effect on a system.

  Procedure (Linux – iptables):
  - Check current rules: sudo iptables -L
  - Block incoming SSH traffic: sudo iptables -A INPUT -p tcp --dport 22 -j DROP
  - Allow HTTP traffic: sudo iptables -A INPUT -p tcp --dport 80 -j ACCEPT
  - Save and verify rules.

(Windows):

- Go to "Windows Defender Firewall"
- Add a new inbound rule to block a port (e.g., 21 for FTP)
- Create another rule to allow port 443 (HTTPS)

Test using telnet, nmap, or browser to verify the effects.

- Expected Outcome: Learn how firewalls control network access and how rules can be created to filter traffic by port or protocol.
- **Tools Required:**
  - Linux terminal or Windows Firewall GUI
  - Admin access
  - Nmap/telnet (for testing)

EXPERIMENT 9: PACKET SNIFFING WITH WIRESHARK

- **Objective:** To capture and analyze live network packets using Wireshark, comparing encrypted (HTTPS) and unencrypted (HTTP) traffic.
- **Procedure:**
  - Install and open Wireshark. Select the active network interface.
  - Start capturing packets.
  - Visit a website using HTTP (e.g., http://example.com) and then one using HTTPS (https://google.com).
  - Stop the capture. Use filters like http or tcp.port == 80 to isolate HTTP traffic.
  - Inspect the packet contents. You will be able to read HTTP headers and plaintext.
  - Filter using tls to inspect encrypted traffic. Notice that HTTPS data is not readable.
- Expected Outcome: Understand the importance of encryption in securing web traffic and how tools like Wireshark can be used to monitor networks.
- Tools Required:
  - Wireshark
  - Internet browser
  - Network access

EXPERIMENT 10: SQL INJECTION AND MITIGATION

- **Objective:** To demonstrate a SQL injection attack on a test web form and secure the input using prepared statements.
- **Procedure:** Create a simple login form using HTML and PHP connected to MySQL. Use the following vulnerable query:

$sql = "SELECT * FROM users WHERE username='$user' AND password='$pass'";

Now, in the login form, enter:

- Username: ' OR '1'='1
- Password: anything

This should bypass the login. To fix it, use prepared statements:

$stmt = $conn->prepare("SELECT * FROM users WHERE username=? AND password=?");

$stmt->bind_param("ss," $user, $pass);

$stmt->execute();

Test again and verify that SQL injection no longer works.

- **Expected Outcome:** Understand how SQL injection works and how prepared statements defend against it.
- **Tools Required:**
  - XAMPP/WAMP
  - PHP, MySQL
  - HTML editor

INDEX

D

E

F

H

I

U

V

W

Z